LIFE

DECEMBER 22, 1941 **10** CENTS
YEARLY SUBSCRIPTION $4.50

REG. U. S. PAT. OFF.

DAYS OF WRATH

BY JOHN W. DOWER

Three-quarters of a century have passed since Japan's surprise attack on Pearl Harbor on December 7, 1941, and only a few survivors are left to recall that shocking day. Even after they are gone, however, the memory will remain. "Remember Pearl Harbor" is branded on the collective American consciousness.

This is true for many reasons. Pearl Harbor is America's preeminent symbol of innocence and victimization, coupled with "righteous fury," as Henry Luce called it in the essay that opens this volume. Japan's attack propelled the United States out of isolationism. It triggered the country's emergence as a great power in the most devastating war of modern times, a global conflict against Nazism, fascism, and Japanese aggression that ended in thoroughgoing victory. And World War II, in turn, set the stage for American eminence in the postwar world that followed, right up to the present day.

On the surface, December 1941 seems almost quaintly far away. America's war began with battleships (the prime Japanese target at Pearl Harbor) and propeller warplanes. It ended with nuclear weapons. Telephone, telegraph, radio, and newsprint dominated communications—years before television caught on and seemingly eons before today's real-time digital information sharing.

The military and civilian bureaucracy of seven decades ago also was relatively lean compared to the sprawling leviathan that exists today, with no less than seventeen intelligence agencies. Its small size did not prevent it from being riddled with turf wars—not only between the civilian and military sectors, but also within them. These rivalries, such as the friction between the Army and Navy commands in Pearl Harbor, impeded information sharing and were one reason Japan's attack caught the U.S. military by surprise.

The genesis of today's national security state is to be found not just in the mobilization for World War II, but also in early postwar determination never again to be caught unaware by an adversary. But that, tragically and astonishingly, is precisely what *did* happen almost exactly six decades after Pearl Harbor, when

◀ **ON THE DAY AFTER THE ATTACK, STUNNED AMERICANS WERE EAGER FOR ANYTHING** that might shed light on the terrible new world they now inhabited. Here, the Embassy Newsreel theater in New York City was a magnet for passersby hoping to see images from Pearl Harbor or anywhere else that might suddenly have become important.

◄ **IN THE DECEMBER 22, 1941** issue of *Life* magazine, founder and editor Henry R. Luce (1898–1967) (left) penned an article to the American public rallying the country behind the war effort. A larger-than-life personality, Luce is credited with creating the news magazine as we know it, and his zeal for photographic journalism helped turn his publishing empire into one of the most successful and influential news outlets even today.

Islamic terrorists attacked the World Trade Center and the Pentagon on September 11, 2001.

Across the country, newspapers almost instinctively responded to al-Qaeda's atrocity with headlines along the lines of "A New Pearl Harbor!" Caught-by-surprise-again was the message, and its racial subtext was only partially obscured. The attack had come, once again, from non-Western, non-Christian adversaries whose willingness and ability to take great risks had been greatly underestimated.

America responded to the September 11 attack in essentially the same way it did to December 7: by declaring war. In this case, however, the enemy was not a nation, but rather an amorphous and elusive target identified as "terror." At the same time, political leaders and most of the media moved quickly to ensure that one of the darkest responses to Japan's attack was not repeated. It was out of the question, they argued, to even consider rounding up and incarcerating people of Arab or Muslim identity who resided in the United States, as had been done to men, women and children of Japanese ancestry after Pearl Harbor. As addressed in these pages (in chapter 8), this accomplished nothing beyond leaving a great stain on our nation's image and honor.

Most of the reverberation between the two attacks was unfortunately less uplifting than the lesson drawn from the Japanese-American internment. In both instances, a great deal of finger-pointing took place. The intelligence failure of September 11, for example, exposed the fact that possessing a gargantuan intelligence apparatus increased rather than decreased the sort of turf wars that plagued the United States in 1941. At the same time, the war on terror made painfully clear that—unlike in World War II—possessing vastly superior military might was no guarantee of victory.

For Americans, World War II ended in less than four years (December 1941 to August 1945). The war on terror has dragged on for 15 years as this book goes to press, still with no end in sight. The world in which war pitted nation-state against nation-state has been replaced by irregular warfare involving non-state antagonists.

Beginning in 1942, the Hollywood director Frank Capra produced a run of "Why We Fight" films for the U.S. Army with series titles like "Know Your Enemy." Pearl Harbor had revealed that it was not just recruits and ordinary citizens who failed to "know the enemy," but top leaders as well. The same can be said of September 11. In 1941, this was true of the Japanese side as well.

Tactically, Pearl Harbor was a brilliant victory on Japan's part. To send six aircraft carriers, more than 350 attack planes, and a supporting fleet of warships across the Pacific without being detected was a stunning accomplishment. It was also strategic folly. Even Admiral Yamamoto Isoroku, who planned the attack and is often quoted as warning that Japan could sustain war against the materially superior United States only for a limited time, was carried away by hubris. The aim of a surprise attack, he told Japan's navy minister, was "to fiercely attack and destroy the U.S. main fleet at the outset of the war, so that the morale of the U.S. Navy and her people goes down to such an extent that it cannot be recovered." This, it was hoped, would ensure some sort of termination of hostilities that left Japan in control of its strategic conquests in Southeast Asia.

The attack did just the opposite, of course. But as we know from other secret records of Japan's war planners, it was possible to marshal all sorts of rational arguments

LIFE

Volume 11, No. 25

December 22, 1941

THE DAY OF WRATH

by HENRY R. LUCE

EDITOR OF LIFE AND TIME

This is the day of wrath. The disaster which befell America on Dec. 7, 1941 was an episode. But it was also a sign. It was a sign of all the weakness and wrongness of American life in recent years. The thousand-odd dead at Pearl Harbor that first day were not merely the victims of Japanese treachery. They were the victims also of a weak and faltering America that had lost its way and failed the world in leadership.

We have come to the end, now, of as pusillanimous an epoch as there ever was in the history of a great people: the twenty years of American history between 1921 and 1941. It is not even possible to call these years tragic, for tragedy implies at least the dignity of fate. And there was no dignity in these years, and nothing of fate that we did not bring upon ourselves. The epoch that is closing was much less tragic than it was shameful.

The President says we have learned a lesson. Some people think he means that we have learned that the Japanese (as now constituted) are a treacherous and dangerous people. But if that is the only lesson we have learned, then God knows what agonies we shall have to undergo before we learn the lessons we have got to learn.

We *will* learn. Every American, not excepting Mr. Roosevelt, now faces the deepest necessity of his life—the necessity of learning that he must find a spiritual rebirth or lose his soul alive. "Still stands Thine ancient sacrifice, an humble and a contrite heart." It is not enough for us at home to say: "Okay, let's go!" as if we could forget the past by one easy act of renunciation.

We will learn these things. Looking at the past, we know that we have not been worthy of ourselves—but looking at the future we know that we can and will be a better people than we have been. We know, too, that however we have misused it, we are the principal trustees in this century of a great heritage of human freedom under God. And therefore we must have victory. We must have victory for the faith of our fathers and for the hope of our young people and our children.

We have still at this moment all—or *almost* all—that is needed for victory. We have, first of all, the young men and young women of America. Despite the meanness of the spiritual environment which we have recently provided them, the strength of this land is in their hearts. We have natural wealth in more abundance than any other nation. We have our American scientists and engineers who stand ready to serve us with their knowledge and their creative toil. We have now, as major allies, Britain and China, two nations bound closer to us by the things of the spirit than any bond that Hitler can forge with terror. We have common military interests with Russia and the chance to build a new bridge between a changing Russia and a changing West. We are seeing Pan-Americanism become a fact and not a phrase. We have other allies of deathless gallantry—in conquered countries and elsewhere.

All these are good things, great things. We have others. We have already the example of heroism of our soldiers and sailors in the far islands of the Pacific. We have at home the greatest productive ability and capacity in the world—in many ways a greater ability and capacity than all the rest of the world put together.

What then do we lack? In this first hour of common counsel in an aroused nation, it is necessary to concentrate first on two things. We lack good organization. And we lack unity.

Victory depends on the whole people. But it begins with leadership—for organization begins with leadership. It is no use to have the greatest resources, the best workers and the ablest managers in the world—if resources, workers and managers are not linked together in clear and dynamic organization which provides for both initiative and control.

We are fortunate that we have done what we have done, that many ships are on the ways, that great factories are built and being built, that we have trained fliers and soldiers and sailors. But the fact is that we haven't done enough—nor done this vast job well enough. And the principal reason is that the organization of our war-effort has not been good. It has been poor.

All that is past. There is no demand for anyone's head. Every man in Washington will be working harder today than he did before Dec. 7—and doing better than he knows how. But it must be insisted that there be no "freezing" of the existing management simply to "save face" or to "spare someone's feelings"—or for political reasons. If some men are not equal to the terrific jobs assigned to them—and there are such—both kindness and patriotism demand that they be given more suitable tasks. If better men can be found—and they can—they must be used.

But quality of personnel—vital though it is—is of less importance than correct organization. Our war-effort has not been correctly organized. It must be correctly organized—at once.

And now what about unity? Are we united? Are we resolved? We all say the same hearty, manly-sounding things. What, then, makes our brave words sound a trifle hollow, and our rage carry a slight suggestion of impotence?

What we lack, still, is a brave acceptance of our terrible reality. We demand victory, but the price of it, in risk, hardship, pain, adventure, is not yet clear to us. The high resolve is yet to come to us that it would be better to leave America a heap of smoking stones than surrender it to the mechanized medievalism which is the Mikado or to the anti-Christ which is Hitler.

This lack of resolve is not surprising. The actual destruction of the American nation by a force outside has seemed fantastic. But it is not fantastic now. It could happen. And America will never win this war against the forces of evil until Americans in every walk of life are gripped at the throat by the realization that *we can lose the war*. For three years we *have* been losing it. When we realize that—then, only then, our own righteous fury will be unloosed.

We must cultivate that realization, and all the resolves that go with it. For the day is not coming; the day is come. It is the day we have all dreaded, yet known in our secret hearts it was our inescapable duty to meet when the world attack on freedom finally came home to us.

This is the day of wrath. It is also the day of hope. For this is the day that Churchill described to the people of Britain in their own blackest hour: the day when "the New World, with all its power and might, steps forth to the rescue and the liberation of the old." Now at last the issue is inexorably joined: either our ideals as free men shall dominate in this century, or the pitiless bayonets of our enemies will.

We have lost something of our power and might. But now at last our battleground is the whole world. The whole world is now our battle-stake. What we have temporarily lost in might we will gain forever in vision and resolve.

For this hour America was made. Uniquely among the nations, America was created out of the hopes of mankind and dedicated to the fulfillment of those hopes. It is for this reason that we accept only two alternatives—either to die in the smoking ruins of a totally destroyed America or else to justify forever the faith of our fathers and the hopes of mankind.

Years ago Woodrow Wilson begged us not to "break the great heart of the world." We go forth now from a half-beleaguered continent to join hands with all men everywhere and by our character and our deeds to write with them the happy and triumphant songs of a new world.

* * *

These are brave words, brave resolves. If our 130 million people truly believe them, no combination of our enemies or their resources, nor any hazards of war, can cheat us of victory.

There is terrible fighting to be done. Every true American will rise to take military arms or civilian action to seize conclusive victory.

There is terrible fighting to be done. All of us will be in the fight—men, women and children, for this is indeed total war. But let us never forget that the hardest fighting is done at the front by our soldiers and sailors.

We have fighting men in the field and on the high seas. Thousands of soldiers and sailors in the Pacific are at this very hour facing death. We tell ourselves how young they are, how gallant, how brave. We salute with our hearts in our throats, tears in our eyes—pray for them too. But also—day after day we must be asking ourselves how good a chance we here at home are giving them to fight and live on. Are we straining every last nerve to see that help, arms, material reach them as soon as possible? If they die (or thousands more like them in the long hard days to come) will they die *through any fault of ours?*

Democracies are always "inefficient," are they? Then let's get it said: This inefficiency cherished in times of war is another word for manslaughter, if not murder. To the extent that we coddle it from here out in ourselves, in high places or low, we're making our own soldiers in the field the cannon fodder of a barbarous and indecent complacency.

In the great fog of battle, we cannot see our soldiers, where they fight or how. We know they fight with every ounce of guts a good American has. And that's plenty. But as we cannot see them in the fog of battle, they cannot see us. When the fog lifts, in the days to come, let us see to it that they look upon us, here at home, and can say as honestly to us as we say to them, "Good going, boys." That will be the day of victory and of peace in our hearts.

as to why the United States would cave in. Many of these arguments, indeed, echo Henry Luce's harshly critical view of pre–Pearl Harbor America's "pusillanimous" decadence, isolationist sentiments, and lack of unity and competent organization.

To these, Japan's wishful strategists added further reasons for looking forward to success. Germany would prevail against England and the Soviet Union. The United States would find it difficult to mount a two-front war in Europe and Asia. Sentiment favoring appeasement was known to exist among some American leaders, who saw Japan as a natural "stabilizing force" against the spread of communism in Asia. Japan's fighting forces were huge and seasoned by combat in China. And when push came

to shove, the esprit de corps of the emperor's loyal soldiers and sailors would be more than sufficient to overcome America's material superiority.

The rationalists and erstwhile realists, whatever their country or culture, are always gifted in argumentation, but all too often lacking in common sense. In 1941, the American underestimation of Japan's intentions and capabilities led to the tragedy so thoroughly and graphically depicted in the following pages. On the opposite side, we see here a stunning Japanese tactical victory, but one that signaled a far greater miscalculation and tragedy for the aggressors. Within just a few years, the fires and billowing black smoke that are our enduring image of Pearl Harbor were transferred to city after city in Japan.

▲ **INVASION FEVER SPREAD ACROSS THE COUNTRY, PARTICULARLY along the coasts. Note the headline in this December 9, edition of New York's *The Sun*.**

MBEAT

"How fortunate for governments that the people they administer don't think."

— ADOLF HITLER

The accords of Versailles, drawn up in the aftermath of World War I, so severely punished Germany that the response was bound to go beyond resentment. Eventually there would be small rebellions at the least, perhaps even stabs at revolution. These things did come to pass, but no one could have foreseen that from the ashes of the Great War an Adolf Hitler would rise. He seemed, by turns, a loser, a petty radical, a thug, a threat and, finally, a vanquishing force to be dealt with. Yet by the time democracies paid Hitler the attention he required, it was too late. With Hitler marching, the world was being violently and forever altered. And as he set fire after fire throughout Europe, America was drawn ever closer to the flames.

The first seeds of World War II were sown on June 28, 1919, when France and Britain carried the day and their version of the Treaty of Versailles was signed by representatives of the Great War's victors. Any conciliation offered by U.S. President Woodrow Wilson was scorned—even mocked—because Europe's two standing powers wanted not merely peace but punishment. They carved up Germany, ceding Czechoslovakia, for example, the Sudetenland, a large part of which clearly wished to stay German because it was German—in heritage, language and blood. Then England and France sought to wreck what remained of Germany by ordering monetary reparations that were as heedless of consequences as they were impossible to meet. "The policy of reducing Germany to servitude for a generation, of depriving a whole nation of happiness should be abhorrent and detestable," the economist John Maynard Keynes wrote one year after the treaty was signed. France and Britain said the policy represented just deserts.

However, while the Versailles pact was meant to all but vaporize the German state, it had precisely the opposite effect.

Germany, careening toward economic collapse, grew desperate. Wild inflation brought down the Weimar Republic, while strikes and socialist revolts erupted throughout the land. Various saviors put themselves forth, but none matched the charisma, will and message of

(Previous Page) **THE NAZIS were obsessed with military panoply and symbolism, a fact much in evidence when Der Führer saluted the crowd in Adolf Hitler Platz during the Nuremberg Reich's Party Congress in 1938. Pageantry also played a big role in the Nazi propaganda machine.**

▶ **GERMAN TROOPS MARCHED closer to war when they entered Czechoslovakia in October 1938, just days after the Munich agreement, whereby Britain and France ceded the Czech region of Sudetenland to Germany. Eight months earlier, Hitler had annexed Austria, then turned his attention to the Sudeten area.**

HULTON/KEYSTONE/GETTY

SOVFOTO

▲ GERMAN BOMBERS BLASTED WARSAW IN SEPTEMBER 1939,
marking the advent of World War II. The Poles, caught off-guard by the
blitzkrieg tactics, fought valiantly but to no avail. By the end of the year,
Germany and the Soviet Union had divided Poland between them.

Adolf Hitler. A Great War veteran who said that Germany's way out of its quagmire was defense, defiance and national pride, he laid claim in his speeches to land that had been reapportioned. Versailles had stipulated for Germany a maximum of 100,000 standing troops and no air force. Hitler, having been named chancellor in 1933—a month before Franklin D. Roosevelt was sworn in as U.S. president—rearmed, blatantly snubbing the accords. The League of Nations in general, and Britain and France in particular, did nothing to stop him, consumed as they were with their own economic troubles. Suddenly Hitler, and a reborn Germany, were at the table.

September 1, 1939: Germany invaded Poland; two days later, France and Britain declared war on Germany. Two weeks later, the Soviet Union, which had recently entered into a nonaggression pact with Hitler, also invaded Poland. The country was taken by month's end.

While Japan was busy extending its dominion in the East, Germany and the U.S.S.R. had designs on all of Europe. In November 1939, Moscow began waging the Winter War in Finland and was victorious by spring. Between April and early June, Germany swept through Denmark, Norway, the Netherlands and Belgium. Both aggressors heard, if faintly, protests from America—a moral embargo against the Soviets, scoldings for Hitler—but they also read the foreign polls, which showed that more than half of the U.S. public didn't want to offer even financial assistance to the besieged nations. Hitler wasn't worried about American intervention in the war because the U.S. military, like its society, was weak by nature, polluted, as he saw it, by African and Jewish blood.

Germany's troops were poised at the Maginot Line, the supposedly impregnable defensive fortifications on France's northeastern border. On May 10, 1940, Prime Minister Neville Chamberlain of Great Britain resigned; his earlier appeasement of Hitler had proved a disaster. Winston Churchill became the commonwealth's leader, declaring, "I have nothing to offer but blood, toil, tears and sweat." Over the next several years, the U.S. and Great Britain would both be fortunate to have leaders who, when the going got tough, could offer inspiration, determination and courage.

AXIS AGGRESSORS

EACH MAN CALLED HIMSELF THE LEADER: **Benito Mussolini** was Il Duce, and **Adolf Hitler** was Der Führer. These longtime dictators of Japan's two partners in the Axis (a term coined by Mussolini) had more than a name in common. Hitler came to power in 1933, 11 years later than Mussolini, whom he deeply admired. Both had made rapid ascents in countries that once flourished mightily but, in the wake of World War I, were left shattered physically and spiritually.

To reverse their nations' fortunes, both men resorted to—and became synonymous with—fascism. They attained their goals with armies of brown- and black-shirted goons who devoured their brilliant oratory, which was malevolent and often erroneous yet hypnotically dramatic and vibrant. As heads of state they enjoyed some early success, notably in creating employment that helped overcome widespread poverty, but their frenzied xenophobia and racism (traits equally abundant in Tokyo) overshadowed their achievements.

For a while, Mussolini was cool to entering into a drawn-out conflict; when he saw the spoils of war accruing to Hitler, however, he caught the fever and, in 1940, dragged his unprepared country into the fray. Mussolini's desire to be the next Caesar would lead to a gruesome public display of his corpse in a Milan square. Hitler's need to be greater than any Caesar would lead to a seedy Berlin bunker and some charred remains.

BLOOD BROTHERS
Hitler and Mussolini enjoyed a motor tour of Florence, Italy, in May 1938.

the least risk now and the greatest hope for world peace in the future.... We must be the great arsenal of democracy."

The speech had a galvanizing effect; suddenly a majority of the American public would risk the consequences of heightened involvement (short of a commitment of troops) in order to support Britain. The course that Roosevelt advocated, in the near term, was made manifest as House Bill 1776—the "Declaration of Interdependence" or, more commonly, Lend-Lease. Even if U.S. soldiers wouldn't yet march off to war, U.S. munitions would, in quantity. As ships and guns arrived in England, Churchill called Lend-Lease a "new Magna Carta."

By 1940, Japan, knowing that it was embarking on risky business in the Pacific, had secured for itself a place in the Tripartite Pact with Germany and Italy. Under the terms of the deal, if any of the partners were attacked by a nation not yet in the war, the others would hurry to its aid. Thus the Axis was formed.

The Allies, in the meantime, were also joined by another major partner. On June 22, Hitler stunned the world by roaring into Russia—breaking his nonaggression pact. A month later the Luftwaffe was raking Moscow from the air. All summer and through the fall, the Nazis pressed on, winning battle after battle, overrunning towns, taking as many as 2 million Russians prisoner. By late 1941, the fascists had under their boots more than 330 million people in a region that stretched from the west coast of Spain to the outskirts of Moscow.

Britain, however, survived. The Blitz had failed—the first slowing of the German march. There was still a chance, Churchill felt—if only America would enter the war.

Even as the U.S. Congress debated repeal of the 1939 Neutrality Act in autumn 1941, a U.S. destroyer, the *Kearny*, was torpedoed in the Atlantic by a German U-boat and limped back to port. Although there had been earlier torpedo and depth-charge exchanges involving American ships, Roosevelt said, ominously, "History has recorded who fired the first shot." But the *Kearny* incident was not enough. The United States would be drawn into the war only by something much bigger.

▶ IN AUGUST 1941, OFF THE COAST OF NEWFOUNDLAND, FDR and Churchill met for the first time, and the prime minister again pressed for aid. Churchill would later say, "No lover ever studied every whim of his mistress as I did those of President Roosevelt." They bade farewell aboard the U.S.S. *Augusta*, before the British leader was piped over the side.

HE EAST

n the 1930s, Japan had its own expansionist intentions—in China, first, then deep into the Pacific. The vastness of the empire's reach led, by necessity, to partnerships. Well before bombs fell upon Pearl Harbor, Japan was formally aligned with Germany. In certain geopolitical ways having to do with global domination, the alliance made sense. In others, it seemed unnatural. The Japanese were clasped in an embrace with a Reich that preached the superiority and the inevitable ascension of the Aryan race. But as the 1940s loomed, the world's nations were not choosing sides strictly on the basis of philosophy. Other issues were more pressing: How can I best survive and keep my family safe? How will my life be affected by whomever I side with? And of course, who's already in my backyard, knocking at the door?

The warrior ethos was deeply ingrained in Japan well before the 20th century. Ancient traditions exalted the samurai. The purity of the nobleman's code of combat was diluted in the late 1800s when modernized armies blended Western weaponry and technology with Japanese principles of courage, fierceness and willingness to fight to the death. Some lamented the dilution of the samurai philosophy, but Japan's new hybrid war machine was extremely effective. In 1905 it defeated Russia in a war for Manchuria and Korea and within five years was showing might on the seas in armored ships. Japan had sided with the Allies in the First World War, but when Britain and France redrew boundaries in Europe and Asia, Japan was upset by the limits of its new dominion. Beginning in the early 1920s, the island nation began flexing its muscles, spending large

(Previous Page) **IN JULY 1938, JAPANESE TROOPS INVADED A village in China's Anhul province. Japan already controlled China's main cities and much of its coast line.**
(Left) **Japanese schoolchildren practiced signaling.**

from

es of

9840
第九年十二月
85

▲ **MARINES HEADED INTO BATTLE IN SHANGHAI. AFTER THAT**
city fell in November 1937, Japan attacked and took the Chinese
capital at Nanjing. The destruction of the city and the rampage of
murder and rape of its inhabitants remains one of the most horrific
war crimes committed.

amounts of money in an attempt to build the world's largest naval air force.

In 1931 the empire launched its undeclared war on China's heartland by extending its reach in Manchuria, which it renamed Manchukuo. Chinese soldiers, debilitated by the war between Mao Zedong's communists and Chiang Kai-shek's Nationalists, were unable to resist as, throughout the decade, Japan pushed south through Beijing and on toward Shanghai. Four qualities invariably marked the Japanese attack: efficiency, discipline, brutality, and, especially, surprise. John Paul Jones once observed, "whoever can surprise well must conquer." The spirit of this maxim informed everything that Japan did militarily up to, and certainly including, Pearl Harbor.

In the years leading to 1941, Japan's intentions were to dominate China and then expand its empire where it might. Initial targets beyond Manchuria included the eastern Chinese cities and Mongolia, but it soon became evident that Japan needed additional resources to fuel its burgeoning campaign. New targets were chosen, including mineral-rich Indochina and oil-rich Indonesia, colonies of France and Holland. With the 1940 German victories over the European mother countries, these Pacific outposts seemed ripe for picking.

In the summer of that year, the Japanese government, which was dominated by militarists—most prominently, War Minister Tojo Hideki, a man described as "the fiercest hawk in the Orient"—decided that the future should include an alliance with Germany, an effort to resume trade with the U.S. (which had been halted by Washington to protest Japan's incursions in China and elsewhere in the Far East) and an offensive in Southeast Asia. As dealmakers flew to Europe and negotiators to America, fighter planes and bombers were readied for sorties in the Pacific.

Tensions between the U.S. and Japan over China continued to worsen. Early in the new year, on January 7, 1941, Adm. Yamamoto Isoroku, commander in chief of Japan's combined fleet, offered his "Views on Preparations for War." The plans included a strategy that stunned most of his colleagues and confirmed the appraisal of one of them that Yamamoto had "a gambler's heart." The big wager in Yamamoto's "Views" was that a surprise attack on the U.S. fleet at Pearl Harbor could result in a quick victory, which would prompt the U.S. to petition for peace in the Pacific. Yamamoto never anticipated a surrender—he wasn't seeking one, nor did he feel that Japan would necessarily prevail

◀ IN 1937, A CRYING INFANT WAS ALL THAT SEEMED TO SURVIVE a Japanese air raid on Shanghai's South Railway Station. Shanghai, China's most important industrial and business center and the site of its largest port, was especially coveted by Tokyo. The last remaining Western-controlled sectors were taken by Japan on December 8, 1941—even as it attacked Pearl Harbor.

in a drawn-out war with America—but he looked rather for a settlement that would allow Japan to pursue its prospecting in Sumatra, Borneo, Java and French Indochina.

Within three weeks of Yamamoto's presentation, U.S. Ambassador to Japan Joseph C. Grew heard a disquieting rumor. He cabled Washington: "My Peruvian colleague told a member of my staff that he had heard from many sources including a Japanese source that the Japanese military forces planned, in the event of trouble with the United States, to attempt a surprise mass attack on Pearl Harbor using all their military facilities." Warnings about Pearl Harbor's vulnerability were nothing new. As early as 1924,

Brig. Gen. Billy Mitchell, then assistant chief of the Army Air Service, had returned from an inspection tour to report that Pacific defenses were inadequate and even to predict that, if the Japanese were to attack Oahu, they would do well to begin with Ford Island at 7:30 in the morning. A January 1938 U.S. War Department survey of Pearl Harbor's defenses warned that if the Japanese attacked, they would do so without notice, and "there can be little doubt that the Hawaiian Islands will be the initial scene of action." On January 24, 1941, three days before Grew reported his rumor, Navy Secretary Frank Knox mailed a letter to the command at Pearl Harbor noting that a reexamination of

▲ IN OCTOBER 1940 IN TOKYO, TOJO (CENTER, IN BOOTS) ALONG with German and Italian representatives, toasted the signing of the Axis alliance. The pact made the Japanese willing conspirators in a war that would claim 60 million lives.

THE SON OF HEAVEN

BORN IN 1901 IN TOKYO, LIFE FOR the young crown prince **Hirohito** was often bleak and lonely, despite the obvious amenities. He was not a robust child, and he was nearsighted. His vision remained uncorrected, because in his culture gods had no need for eyeglasses. He was a thoughtful boy with many interests, but the joys of a carefree childhood eluded him; he could only watch from his royal pedestal. It must have been a welcome liberation when, at the age of 19, he became the first Japanese crown prince to travel abroad, where he spent six gloriously normal months in Europe.

Hirohito ascended the Chrysanthemum Throne on December 25, 1926, following the death of his father. Japan at the time was becoming increasingly democratic and internationalist; by the early 1930s, however, a martial influence had swept the country. Some accounts maintain that the emperor was unsympathetic, opposed to both the alliance with Germany and Italy and the prospect of war with the United States. Other historians contend, though, that Hirohito was all along complicit with Japanese expansionist policies. What is clear is that, near the war's end, Hirohito sided with those who sought peace rather than those who wanted to fight to the death. Several of his advisors were tried and convicted of war crimes, but not the emperor. Patrick Lennox Tierney was a staff officer working for Gen. MacArthur, the Supreme Commander of the Allied Powers, and was present on the day in in late 1950 when Hirohito visited the general's offices to make a personal apology for Japan's actions during the war, especially the attack on Pearl Harbor. Tierney recounts how he witnessed what he considered the stunning rudeness of MacArthur's refusal to admit or acknowledge the emperor. Tierney said, "Apology is a very important thing in Japan. With us, we don't apologize unless we get caught with our hand in the cookie jar, but for the Japanese, there is a very strong sense of what an apology means."

In 1946, Hirohito renounced any claims to divinity. In his later years he made frequent public appearances in an effort to reach out to commoners. The man himself was doubtless happiest when indulging in his lifelong interest in marine-biology research, publishing several well-received volumes on his specialty, the jellyfish. The Showa Emperor died in 1989. It was a name he had long ago chosen for his reign. "Showa" means Enlightened Peace.

HIROHITO SHOWED HIS distaste for his government's saber-rattling by expressing the hope that the next prime minister would be "one who has no fascist leanings, and about whom there has been no unsavory rumor, who is moderate in thought and who is not militaristic."

the base's readiness had been undertaken, "prompted by the increased gravity of the situation with respect to Japan, and by reports from abroad of successful bombing and torpedo plane attacks on ships while in bases."

Knox reported the conclusions of the reappraisal: "If war eventuates with Japan, it is believed easily possible that hostilities would be initiated by a surprise attack upon the Fleet or the Naval Base at Pearl Harbor. In my opinion, the inherent possibilities of a major disaster to the Fleet or Naval Base warrant taking every step, as rapidly as can be done, that will increase the joint readiness of the Army and Navy to withstand a raid of the character mentioned above."

"Every step" was not taken, of course: The information supplied by both Knox and Grew, and Mitchell well before them, was largely ignored in Washington. And perhaps that was understandable, since nothing about any surprise attack was turning up in the MAGIC transcripts.

In August 1940, Lt. Col. William F. Friedman of the Army Signal Corps had succeeded in cracking the complex Japanese diplomatic code called PURPLE, and quickly a series of machines, also called PURPLE, had been built and put into action. They translated intercepts of Japanese transmissions between Tokyo and its emissaries in Washington, and the messages, called MAGIC by the Americans, were then circulated among U.S. officials. The U.S. knew about Japan's designs on Southeast Asia but learned nothing from PURPLE about Pearl Harbor. Just so: Throughout 1941, information about the daring assault was so closely held by officials in Tokyo that they apparently kept even their ambassador to the U.S., Nomura Kichisaburo, in the dark.

Japan was not, of course, just a war machine; it was a society as well. It had an emperor. Hirohito was a still-young man in 1941, having taken the throne in 1926 at age 25. He was, essentially, an onlooker to his country's aggression. Out of deference to an ancient system, generals and government officials routinely made presentations to the emperor, but these were hardly consultations. Hirohito and some moderate politicians occasionally issued calls for peace throughout the 1930s and into the '40s. But the emperor was politely ignored by the militarists, and the pols were, one by one, replaced. Civilian government was eroding in Japan, as censorship and propaganda routed any temperate views. The generals succeeded in inflaming a national xenophobia and sense of righteousness.

The last chapter of Japan's march to world war began at one of Hirohito's Imperial Conferences, this one held on September 6, 1941. There, the cabinet officially adopted the military's war plan. The emperor, in turn, read a poem written by his grandfather: "In a world/Where all the seas/Are brethren,/Why do wind and wave/So stridently clash?" A lingering moderate in the government, Prince Konoye Fumimaro, Japan's premier, sensed that the emperor's

▲ **EMPEROR HIROHITO LED AN INSPECTION TOUR IN OSAKA OF** giant listening horns intended to pick up the sound of approaching enemy aircraft. The horns exemplified not only Japan's constant search for the next big technological idea but also the extent of the country's xenophobia in the 1930s.

KYODO NEWS

MAINICHI NEWSPAPERS / AFLO

◀ **IN SEPTEMBER 1940,** people in Osaka took part in an air-raid drill. The precautions would prove prudent when, on April 18, 1942, Lt. Col. Jimmy Doolittle led the first Allied air raid on Tokyo.

▶ **STUDENTS HUDDLED AT A** bomb shelter in Osaka during a drill in October 1941. U.S. air raids would not strike the Japanese mainland with regularity for another three years but by war's end would kill or wound nearly a million people.

mindset might point to an escape from disaster. In a meeting that evening with Ambassador Grew, Konoye requested an audience with President Roosevelt to see whether a peaceful solution could be reached. As Grew took the request to Washington, Konoye asked Yamamoto whether his navy was prepared, should the overture be rebuffed. "If you insist on my going ahead," the admiral replied, "I can promise to give them hell for a year or a year and a half, but can guarantee nothing as to what will happen after that." Yamamoto had been to the U.S. and was worried that the industrial machine there, coupled with the stores of fuel in Texas oil fields, would eventually overwhelm any foe.

Roosevelt, counseled by Secretary of State Cordell Hull, who of course knew of Japan's constant duplicity through the MAGIC dispatches, told the Japanese that summits were pointless without Japanese capitulation on China (and now French Indochina, which Japan had brazenly occupied in midsummer).

On October 16, Konoye resigned as premier. He was succeeded by Tojo, who the previous year had been made minister of war. Soon after, Adm. Nagano Osami approved Yamamoto's Pearl Harbor plan, and a week after that Tojo addressed a meeting of 200 government officials: "We must go on to develop in ever-expanding progression. There is no retreat." On November 17, Yamamoto gave a similar speech to key members of the First Air Fleet aboard the flagship *Agaki*: "Although we hope to achieve surprise, everyone should be prepared for terrific American resistance in this operation." A toast was raised to success in the coming battle: "Banzai! Banzai! Banzai!"

n 1941, a majority of Americans, while sympathetic to the foreign oppressed, reserved their energies for matters close to home. Precious jobs had to be found or maintained, precious food harvested or scrounged. In a nation emerging from the brutal Depression, few citizens wanted any part of another debilitating fight. Extreme isolationists wouldn't even pick sides; most Americans allowed that you could tell good guys from bad and that the U.S. should back the democracies however it could— short of sending our boys. In Washington, President Roosevelt took the public's pulse but also saw where things were headed. He ordered buildup after buildup of arms and men. As November turned to December, he felt that something was about to give.

Prior to December 7, 1941, there was an overarching difference between the United States and its foes, Germany, Italy and Japan. They were already at war, and America wasn't. Yes, there was a sense of emergency, akin to the feeling of wartime, in America: A $1.5 billion increase to upgrade the Army and build more planes in May 1940 was followed by another billion for the Army later that year, plus nearly $700 million for the Navy. On September 16, the first U.S. peacetime draft was instituted. But despite all this building up and battening down, the Neutrality Act still had authority. America wanted, after its experience in World War I, to stay off the battlefield at all costs. Roosevelt could chip away at neutrality and isolationism as much as he wanted with words—words informed by a keen appreciation of where Hitler and Tojo were headed—but he couldn't make his countrymen go to war if they weren't ready to go.

And they wouldn't be ready until their hand was forced. If massive increases in defense spending and armament manufacture told one tale, the polls told another. A survey taken immediately after the 1939 outbreak of war in Europe showed that 30 percent of Americans were still dedicated to complete neutrality and an embargo on all belligerents, while 37 percent favored neutrality with trade allowed on a cash-and-carry basis. Add it up, and you get two-thirds of the U.S. still in favor of neutrality. By June 1940, just after

(Previous Page) **THE OPENING** of an armor-plate factory in Philadelphia in mid-1941 led to this patriotic display. The plant was owned by Henry Disston and Sons, whose usual business was making handsaws. Allocating metal to the war effort was a crucial part of the nation's ability to supply the military with necessary equipment. Metal shortages meant that most metal consumer items were unavailable to the public.

▶ **MASSACHUSETTS WOMEN'S** Political Club members paid a visit to the White House on February 25, 1941, to present a petition decrying the Lend-Lease agreement. That the Depression, and even World War I, weren't far removed from the public mind was never lost on FDR. The president contended, however, that "the best immediate defense of the United States is the success of Great Britain defending itself."

BROWN BROTHERS

Italy declared war, 67 percent of Americans were in favor of aiding the Allies, but only 27 percent were prepared to go to war. A month later this number had fallen to 15 percent. To secure reelection to a historic third term in 1940, Roosevelt ran on a plank that promised to keep America out of the war. Even as comic-strip hero Joe Palooka was urging his manager Knobby Walsh to spend $10,000 on savings bonds instead of a race horse, an October 1941 Gallup Poll showed that a majority of Americans had no intention to buy savings bonds or stamps. At the same time, a poll by *Fortune* magazine found that people were concerned that the future would bring higher prices, fewer jobs and fewer opportunities for their children. These were the big issues.

So the United States was living two lives: the political, which saw entry into the world war, in some fashion, as an inevitability, and the day-to-day, which fully realized there was a threat but dared to hope that war could be avoided.

The man straddling the gulf was Roosevelt. He was by no means a hawk, but he was a realist, and he was receiving real information each day not only from his generals but also from Secretary of State Cordell Hull, a smart and tough man open to negotiation when it might bear fruit but ready to resort to other means when talking proved fruitless. Roosevelt and Hull knew they were dealing with a public that generally didn't want to fight and that included a strong minority—a minority that would remain vocal through December 6, 1941—that wanted America to stay out of war, come what may.

Very few American isolationists sided with the Nazis, and there was no thinking that Japan should rule China. But most isolationists believed that the wars in Europe and Asia were not their country's affair. Europe was an old, always warring place—a place that Americans had left. Moreover, battered by the Depression, Americans were having no easy time propping up their own nation. The United States should not get involved in the tribal feuds of ancestors (went the reasoning). And it could not—not at that moment. Furthermore, citizens and generals had

HULTON/KEYSTONE/GETTY

◄ **DURING A WORLDWIDE** broadcast on May 27, 1941, FDR proclaimed "that an unlimited national emergency confronts this country, which requires that its military, naval, air and civilian defenses [be readied] to repel any and all acts or threats of aggression." Sen. Burton Wheeler replied that Roosevelt was "preaching fear."

LAST-DITCH EFFORTS

IN THE NINE MONTHS LEADING TO BLOODY Sunday, Secretary of State **Cordell Hull** met 40 times with Japanese ambassador **Nomura Kichisaburo**. The two men failed, of course, to prevent war, but their talks have long been grist for historians.

Hull's reputation—built over 11 years and nine months on the job, then topped with the Nobel Peace Prize in 1945—is that of a peacemaker who was clear-eyed about war. In the 1930s, he scored a resounding success with his Good Neighbor Policy in Latin America, and his diplomacy fostered a united front of American countries against the Axis. Regarding Japan, his record is less certain. Some historians credit him with great patience as he tried to strengthen the position of Japanese moderates. Others maintain that Hull's penchant for sermonizing and ceaseless deliberation ultimately served him poorly in the attempt to avoid war in the Pacific.

Concerning Nomura, the question was whether he bargained in good faith: Did he know about the planned sneak attack? Japan's final memorandum was handed to Hull at 2:20 p.m. on December 7—one hour after the launch of the attack. But even if Hull had received it earlier, there was no ultimatum in it, only a hint: "The Japanese government regrets to have to notify hereby the American government that in view of the attitude of the American government, it cannot but consider that it is impossible to reach an agreement through further negotiations." Subsequent research, however, has uncovered an earlier memo written by the Japanese Foreign Ministry, dated December 3, 1941, the last paragraph of which left no question about the Japanese intentions: "The government of the United States of America has not shown even the slightest degree of sincerity in the current negotiations, and the Japanese government regrets to have to solemnly notify hereby your government that we are forced to terminate negotiations, recognizing that the continuation of talks will in no way contribute to the stability of East Asia, and that you will be held responsible for any and all the consequences that may arise in the future."

This last part of the paragraph was tantamount to a declaration of war. Who was responsible for the deceit implicit in the tampering with the memos? In 2010, Takeo Iguchi, professor emeritus at Shobi University and former ambassador to New Zealand, published a book called *Demystifying Pearl Harbor: A New Perspective from Japan*, in which he revealed his exhaustive research about the events leading up to the Day of Infamy. Iguchi had been a boy of 11 that day, the son of a counselor at the Japanese Embassy in Washington. His life's work has been to prove that the stigma Japan has borne of having perpetrated a "sneak attack" is the result of the Japanese military's having kept the Japanese embassy in the dark as to the contents of the memorandum intended for Secretary of State Cordell Hull and the timing of its delivery.

By the time this came to light, however, it was too late for the hapless Nomura. On December 7, Hull excoriated him for his deceit, and the image of the treacherous ambassador was firmly lodged in America's wartime craw.

SECRETARY OF STATE HULL escorted Ambassador Nomura (left) and special envoy Kurusu Saburo to the White House on November 17, 1941.

all seen how the U.S. had pitched in at the eleventh hour to help Britain and France win the Great War only to find American recommendations at Versailles snubbed. Would the Yanks bail them out again, at blood cost, and again get nothing in return?

These arguments seemed reasonable throughout the 1930s and eventually coalesced into formal associations. The Committee to Defend America by Aiding the Allies said that the U.S. should remain neutral but assist Great Britain: A British victory would keep the world a stable place, safe for democracies. This sounded like double-speak to the America First Committee, which insisted that it was more important to stay out of the war than to try to back either horse.

America Firsters grew to be 800,000 in number. One among them was transcendentally famous and influential. This was Charles A. Lindbergh, the great hero of the air. His popularity in America since his solo flight across the Atlantic in 1927 had never waned; if anything, it had increased after the 1932 kidnapping and murder of his first son. He was a celebrity of the highest magnitude. Lucky Lindy was a national institution.

Then, after several visits to Nazi Germany, Lucky Lindy told his countrymen that intervention was not only wrong

▲ LINDBERGH INSPECTED AN AIRPLANE PLANT IN BREMEN, Germany, in 1936, and spoke at an America First rally (left) in Chicago in April 1941. A week later, columnist-with-clout Walter Winchell said of a similar gathering: "More American flags than Americans."

from a philosophical standpoint but unwise from a military one. The Luftwaffe was one strong flying machine, Lindbergh reported, and the Germans really knew how to get things done.

Lindbergh was not necessarily a Nazi sympathizer, but he was a man of firm opinions and, throughout the 1930s and into the '40s, a man of mistakes. On one visit to Germany, he attended a stag dinner hosted by Hitler henchman Hermann Goering, and during the festivities Lindbergh accepted a medal. Later that night he showed it to his wife, Anne Morrow Lindbergh, who saw it for what it would become and said quietly, "the albatross."

Remaining polite while accepting a medal might have been explained away, but the Des Moines speech could not be. There, in September 1941, Lindbergh spoke the words—words his wife warned him not to utter—that reflected a philosophy that would forever tarnish his image and would, in the near term, soil the America First movement. Addressing a crowd of like thinkers, Lindbergh proclaimed that the British government, the Roosevelt administration

and "the Jews" were spoiling for intervention—and he could understand that, since it was their constituencies at risk—but that Americans should see these "war agitators" for what they were, and oppose them.

This was a problem. Are we not all Americans? asked many of Lindbergh's countrymen. And, of course, the bit about the Jews smacked of anti-Semitism, which in 1941 was a very short leap from Nazism. With the possibility of war looming larger every day, Lindbergh had laid himself—and his movement—open to fierce criticism. Roosevelt publicly denounced him. Lindbergh countered by resigning his commission in the Army Air Corps Reserve. (Only weeks later, with Pearl Harbor smoldering, he would try to reenlist but would be turned down.)

If isolationists came in several stripes and degrees of intensity and were inspired in their cause by every emotion from abject fear to racial bigotry, then those who admitted to being interventionists came in one kind only. They saw Hitler's march as an evil thing—a totalitarian purge of Europe's free societies. They worried that it might become

an effort at world domination. Because the Japanese were in league with the Germans, they were part of the equation, the product of which could be a world controlled by Hitler (and maybe Mussolini) in the West, Tojo in the East.

But intervention equated, from day one, with American death—and so it was insupportable to most.

Thus was the country split, with the majority favoring an opposition to Hitler, a measured support of European democracies and every effort not to send our boys to the battlefield. On December 7 this massive part of the populace, having been primed over time by Roosevelt, would shout out loud: Let's go get 'em. Or, as Sen. Burton K. Wheeler, who awoke that day a fervent isolationist, put it: "The only thing now to do is to lick hell out of them."

So how did this interesting political situation impact the day-to-day? Greatly, and in graphic ways. In America in 1941, fear had purchase, and fatalism, sometimes manifested as a let's-dance-while-we-can denial, was in the air. "Two-fifths of our people are more interested in the baseball scores than they are in foreign news," wrote William Allen White in the *Emporia Gazette* as the summer wound down. And why not? Joe DiMaggio had hit in 56 straight games that magical season, and Ted Williams had batted .406. Joe Louis, heavyweight champ since 1938, whomped seven more members of the Bum of the Month Club in 1941.

Many Americans were reading William L. Shirer's *Berlin Diary*. Many others were reading F. Scott Fitzgerald's posthumously published novel of Hollywood, *The Last Tycoon*. In New York City, Glenn Miller, Benny Goodman, Duke Ellington, Harry James and Guy Lombardo ruled the clubs and ballrooms. Helen Hayes, Ethel Barrymore, Gertrude Lawrence and Danny Kaye were on Broadway in shows by Noel Coward, Lillian Hellman and Cole Porter.

Upstate in the Adirondacks, skiers were practicing for possible military action in Europe. Down in Georgia, vocational schools were teaching young people to build ships, planes and guns. Out in Los Angeles, 6,000 artillerymen were working with their antiaircraft weapons, getting ready for an air-raid drill. In Chicago, paperboys tried to sell war stamps door-to-door.

In the papers during the first week of December, an ad for a sunlamp boosted the benefits of ultraviolet rays, and another said that a carton of cigarettes would make the perfect Christmas gift. Yet another poll indicated that 58 percent of Americans didn't exercise apart from their jobs. The *Boston Globe* had a recommendation for young parents: "Do not punish your child by not allowing him to have his ice cream. Ice cream is a good food and is valuable for both energy and body building." Another *Globe* article offered tips for wives: "Don't serve him scrambled newspapers

◄ **THEY WERE STRESSFUL** times, but for indispensables like baseball and romance, there was always room. In late September this Brooklyn bar was ripe for revelry as patrons celebrated the National League pennant their Dodgers had just brought home.

▼ **THIS SEPTEMBER 1941** photo shows the seven Patten brothers—Myrne, Ray, Allen, Bruce, Gilbert, Marvin and Clarence Jr.—who served together on the *Nevada*. Here they hoist their father Clarence after his enlistment in the Navy. All survived the attack.

◄ **SOLDIERS' MORALE SKY-**
rocketed when Hollywood
lovelies led the cheers. A young
Jane Russell at the Army
Air Corps's advanced flying
school on July 11, 1941.

▼ **DOROTHY LAMOUR WAS**
the Army's favorite pinup girl
when she dined, in July 1941,
with these soldiers in Honolulu.
Her remarkable fund-raising
efforts would earn her the
sobriquet Bond Bombshell.

instead of scrambled eggs for breakfast. Don't make a sad
and I-don't-understand-it face when he laughs his head off
over 'the best joke of the century.'"

On Cape Cod, 23,000 new troops arrived at Camp
Edwards while taps sounded in the background. At Filene's
department store, you couldn't get proper stockings because
of the embargo on Japanese silk. A Boston hairdresser was
using cotton thread instead of metal bobby pins to keep a
'do in place.

Anne Morrow Lindbergh, who would eventually
say that her husband had been used by the Nazis, wrote
that week: "Soldiers on the train, searchlights in the sky,
planes maneuvering in threes. All the billboards have gone
'Defense' mad, with pictures of soldiers and sailors on them.
Vogue photographs its models in front of Bundles for Britain
planes. Longchamps has V's done in vegetables in the windows. Elizabeth Arden gets out a V for Victory lipstick." In
magazine ads that first week of December, General Motors
would have Americans believe "Defense Comes First with
Oldsmobile!" and Remington asserted, "Victory Begins at a
Thousand Peaceful Desks."

You could escape the war imagery. At the movies, *Dr. Jekyll and Mr. Hyde*, *Here Comes Mr. Jordan*, *The Maltese Falcon* and *Dumbo* were playing. (On the evening of December 6, however, no one in several cities could see *Two-Faced Woman*, in which Greta Garbo played twin sisters sleeping with the same man, because the Catholic Legion of Decency had earlier won its battle to have the film withdrawn.)

In the nation's capital, Hull learned, from intercepted messages, that Japan had set a firm deadline of November 29

to put its operations into motion. The American government knew, in this first week of December, that something was coming.

LIFE magazine ran a story that week on the Japanese diplomatic efforts, profiling emissaries Kurusu Saburo and Nomura Kichisaburo in an article headlined "Japanese Bow and Grin for the Camera But Get Nowhere in Washington."

Secretary of the Navy Frank Knox released his annual report on December 6, which read in part, "the American people may feel fully confident in their Navy. In my opinion,

U.S.S. ARIZONA MEMORIAL/NPS

the loyalty, morale and technical ability of the personnel are without superior. On any comparable basis, the United States Navy is second to none."

Another poll: The week before Pearl Harbor, according to Gallup, 52 percent of Americans thought the U.S. would go to war against Japan "sometime in the near future." A December 7 headline in the *New York Times*—"Japan Rattles Sword But Echo Is Pianissimo"—was belied by an eerie sense of foreboding that, finally, had touched a majority of Americans. Better to rely not on journalism that weekend but on the horoscope, which predicted "strange, sudden and wholly unpredictable and inexplicable occurrences affecting all phases of life."

In Honolulu on Saturday, officers played golf at the Fort Shafter course. Some 24,000 football fans watched the University of Hawaii Rainbows beat Willamette. After nightfall, sailors cruised Hotel Street, and some of them took in the floor show with the "Tantalizing Tootsies" at the Princess. Elsewhere, there was a dinner at the Pearl Harbor Officers' Club, and a battle of the fleet's dance bands. The winner would compete with the reigning champs from the *Arizona*. The swinging outfit from the *Pennsylvania* won. The next day, after playing for the daily flag-raising ceremony, all twenty-one members of the *Arizona*'s band would die.

On the night of December 6, Lt. Gen. Walter C. Short, commander of the U.S. Army's Hawaiian Department, gazed upon the harbor. He noted the twinkling lights of the battleships and observed, "Isn't that a beautiful sight? And what a target they would make."

▲ **THE BLACK CAT CAFE WAS** a favorite haven for servicemen. Located in Pearl Harbor near Hotel Street, it was officially "off limits" to military personnel, but soldiers still found their way there to buy cheap beer and let off some steam.

▶ **HULA DANCERS PERFORMED** for sailors aboard the U.S.S. *Honolulu* in July 1939. (Following Pages) The annual Christmas lights on Fort Street in Honolulu provided a merry setting. It was only days before the attack on Pearl Harbor would put an end to seasonal cheer.

HAWAII STATE ARCHIVES

4 DECEMBER 7,

1941

dm. Yamamoto called the U.S. fleet at Pearl Harbor "a dagger pointed at our throat." Secretary of State Hull's opinion of Japanese aggression had distilled to a brief statement: "Nothing will stop them but force." Yamamoto's attack was put in motion as Japanese aircraft carriers moved across the Pacific, closing the 3,400 miles between Japan and Hawaii. President Roosevelt could only sit and wait, having determined that the blow that would force America to arms would come from Japan—not Germany—and that the U.S. must let the blow land rather than issue a first strike. The eve of the bombing was an eerie calm before the storm as, for politicians if not for the public, war had already become a reality. The duel was engaged, with guns yet to be fired.

In the last week of November, Japan's deadline to put its attack plan in motion finally arrived. Vice Adm. Nagumo Chuichi assembled the staffs of his carriers, battleships, cruisers, destroyers and submarines, and for the first time revealed to them that their target was Pearl Harbor. They had three days to digest the news; then ships and planes started making their way east-southeast.

Nagumo and his fleet had already been at sea for more than 24 hours when, in Washington, Secretary of State Hull met with Japanese diplomats Nomura Kichisaburo and Kurusu Saburo, who were, it seemed, unaware of the mobilization and the attack plans in general. Hull wanted to discuss America's Ten Points, which amounted to a renewed demand for Japan's withdrawal from China and Indochina as a principal condition for any negotiated peace. Nomura and Kurusu treated the discussions with due seriousness, but if Hull needed confirmation that the talks were largely worthless, he got it on November 29 when he received a copy of a speech Tojo had just given in Japan. While short of a formal declaration of war, the speech was certainly intended to inspire the Japanese military. Hull called Roosevelt, who was vacationing in Warm Springs, Georgia, and, as he later recalled, impressed upon the president "the

(Previous Page) **LOOKING DOWN Battleship Row: The** *California* (left) listed to port after suffering two torpedo hits. The billowing smoke was mainly from the doomed *Arizona*.

▲ **VICE ADM. NAGUMO Chuichi, commander in chief of the First Air Fleet. From the beginning, he was adamant that Yamamoto's plan was riddled with problems.**

▲ **THIS BANQUET ON THE** carrier *Akagi* on November 25, 1941, celebrated the grand mission that lay ahead. Commander Fuchida Mitsuo, who would lead the air attack, is seated at rear, third from right. (Left) A toast was raised on the *Akagi*.

imminent danger of a Japanese attack, and advised him to advance the date of his return to Washington." Roosevelt packed his bags.

On December 1, Japanese land forces swept south through Indochina, while Nagumo's ocean-going task force was now halfway to Hawaii, having crossed the international date line unnoticed. One of Nagumo's aides later remembered the 12-day sail across a "vacant sea" as "the most difficult and most agonizing period for every officer in the Naval General Staff who knew about Pearl Harbor."

While the ships made their quiet way across the Pacific, Japan was in action throughout the globe. In Washington, the Japanese negotiators were trying to keep their American counterparts engaged, promising that an answer to the Ten Points would be forthcoming. In Germany, another ambassador, Oshima Hiroshi, was huddling with Nazi foreign minister Joachim von Ribbentrop, letting the Axis partners know that there existed "extreme danger that

AP

DID ROOSEVELT KNOW?

THE ATTACK ON PEARL HARBOR IS ONE OF the most odious chapters in American history. And of the many questions raised therein, the most unappetizing is one that is heard increasingly: Did President **Franklin Delano Roosevelt** know ahead of time where and when the attack would come?

It is clear that Roosevelt, more than most of his countrymen, recognized early on that Americans would not be able to isolate themselves from the conflict that would become known as World War II. His repeated calls for increased military readiness and for measures such as the Lend-Lease pact show that he considered war to be unavoidable. Such prescience, however, reflects access to classified information rather than any personal desire to enter into an unnecessary fight.

One weapon frequently wielded by revisionists is the fact that, because the U.S. had broken the Japanese PURPLE code long before Pearl Harbor, military intelligence had access to messages that must have alerted them to specific Japanese intentions. Indeed, the intelligence gathering was remarkable, but intelligence that is passed on improperly or ineffectually—or simply not picked up on—is often worse than none whatsoever. It's entirely possible that had the code not been broken, American preparedness would have been better.

It has been more than seven decades since the attack—75 years for countless historians to pore over the material at hand. In his 1999 book, *Day of Deceit: The Truth about FDR and Pearl Harbor*, Robert Stinnett, a naval photographer and journalist, though convinced of the Pearl Harbor conspiracy, is sympathetic regarding FDR's motives. He writes in his book: "As a veteran of the Pacific War, I felt a sense of outrage as I uncovered secrets that had been hidden from Americans for more than fifty years. But I understood the agonizing dilemma faced by President Roosevelt. He was forced to find circuitous means to persuade an isolationist America to join in a fight for freedom." Much has been written, nothing has been proved. In 1941, the idea of the president acting without transparency and accountability was unthinkable. Today, we are accustomed to it. In hindsight, most Americans would probably agree that entering World War II was for the best, even if the push into it might have been questionable.

PRESIDENT ROOSEVELT AND Cordell Hull shared a ride to the White House on August 17, 1941. FDR had just returned from his historic meeting at sea with Churchill.

▲ **IT IS IRONIC THAT YAMAMOTO ISOROKU, THE GRAND MASTER** of the attack plan, was perhaps the one man in Japan who most feared war with the United States. In April 1943, American intelligence learned that he was flying to Bougainville island in the Pacific, and he was shot down by American P-38s.

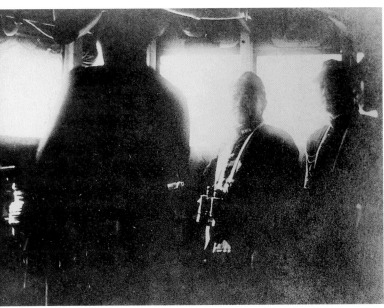

▲ **PHOTOGRAPHED FROM THE FLAGSHIP** *AKAGI,* **THE AIRCRAFT** carrier *Kaga* (top) steamed through heavy seas en route to Pearl Harbor. With typical naval superstition, Japanese sailors regarded the *Kaga* as a "victorious" ship because she had enjoyed success off China in the 1930s. The carrier *Zuikaku* is visible at right. Adm. Nagumo (above, center) stood on the bridge of the *Akagi* as it made for Hawaii.

war may suddenly break out between the Anglo-Saxon nations and Japan through some clash of arms... this war may come quicker than anyone dreams." Ribbentrop assured Oshima, "Should Japan become engaged in a war against the United States, Germany, of course, would join the war immediately. There is absolutely no possibility of Germany's entering into a separate peace with the United States under such circumstances. The Führer is determined on that point."

In Tokyo on December 1, another Imperial Conference was held at Hirohito's palace. After plans were reviewed and Tojo made an impassioned speech, the emperor nodded his head, thereby giving his consent to all-out war. "His Majesty," wrote an observer, "seemed to be in an excellent mood, and we were filled with awe." Later that day, about 940 miles north of the Midway islands, Nagumo received Yamamoto's message to proceed: "Climb Mount Niitaka, 1208." The number referred to the eighth day of the 12th month, which on the Hawaiian side of the international date line would be December 7, 1941.

On December 2 at Pearl Harbor, Adm. Husband E. Kimmel, head of the Navy command, discussed intelligence reports with his aide. He asked Lt. Cdr. Edwin T. Layton for updates on the location of Japan's aircraft carriers. Layton gave estimates for all except the four carriers in Divisions 1 and 2.

"What!" Kimmel said. "You don't know where Carrier Division 1 and Carrier Division 2 are?"

"No, sir, I do not," replied Layton. "I think they are in home waters but I do not know where they are. The rest of these units, I feel pretty confident of their locations."

"Do you mean to say," challenged Kimmel, "that they could be rounding Diamond Head and you wouldn't know it?"

"I hope they would be sighted before now," said Layton.

The next day—Wednesday, December 3—two Japanese communications were intercepted and translated into MAGIC memorandums. The first, already more than two weeks old, directed the Japanese consulate in Honolulu to step up its periodic reports on the location of American warships in Pearl Harbor. The message was seen as not especially important because the Japanese had long been attempting reconnaissance of American naval bases. The second intercept was a reply from Tojo to his ambassadors, who had suggested that war might be averted through a summit conference at "some midway point, such as

ON THEIR WATCH

WITH ANY DISASTER, PARTICULARLY ONE as notorious as Pearl Harbor, there is a rush to judgment. How could it have happened? Who is responsible?

Official investigations began at once with a board of inquiry appointed by President Roosevelt and chaired by Supreme Court Justice Owen J. Roberts. On January 23, 1942, the Roberts Commission found that **Adm. Husband E. Kimmel** (right), commander in chief of the Pacific Fleet, and **Lt. Gen. Walter C. Short** (below right), commanding officer of the Army's Hawaiian Department, were guilty of "dereliction of duty" and "errors of judgment [that] were the effective causes for the success of the attack." (They were later cleared.) Kimmel and Short, who had already been relieved of their commands, retired shortly after Roberts's report was issued.

A half dozen military tribunals were conducted before the war's end, but none had access to all the evidence. Immediately after the war, a congressional investigation was begun; the hearings inspired the same sort of public fascination as Teapot Dome had or Watergate would. Criticism fell upon many, and Kimmel and Short were cleared of dereliction of duty, but they were still blamed for shortcomings. The complete exoneration that the two friends had fought so bitterly for eluded them. Ever since, both men have had staunch supporters who have worked tirelessly to restore their reputations. Indeed, as recently as May 25, 1999, the Senate voted to exonerate them posthumously, but President Clinton declined to sign the measure into law.

The debate all along has turned on what information the two officers had from Washington and how they acted on it. There were warnings on November 27 and earlier, but a warning about war doesn't constitute a warning about an attack. On the other hand, officials in Washington couldn't advise of a Japanese action that they themselves could not accurately predict.

▲ TWO WAVES OF ATTACK AIRPLANES WERE LAUNCHED FROM
the *Akagi* on the morning of December 7, 1941. The Japanese bombers
would cause damage to the *Oklahoma*, *West Virginia* and *California*.

Honolulu." Tojo's answer: "[I]t would be inappropriate for us to propose such a meeting."

Roosevelt tried one last time to petition for peace. On December 6, he drafted a personal appeal to Hirohito and had it encoded and sent, at approximately 9 p.m., to Ambassador Grew in Tokyo. At just about that time, Ambassador Nomura received word in Washington that an answer to the Ten Points was coming immediately in the form of a 14-part memo. In late afternoon and early evening, the first 13 parts of the memo were intercepted, deciphered and sent to Roosevelt. When the president finished reading the items, which included nothing helpful—mostly threats—he said, "This means war."

The 14th part of the Japanese message was not received and circulated in Washington until the morning of December 7, and at that point a follow-up memorandum was also intercepted. Part 14 stated that Japan was terminating diplomatic relations with the United States, and the postscript instructed Ambassador Nomura to deliver the Japanese view to Cordell Hull at 1 o'clock. Realizing that 1 p.m. on the East Coast corresponded to daybreak in the Pacific, intelligence officer Col. Rufus S. Bratton hurriedly sought to warn his superiors of a possible attack.

▶ DECEMBER 7: FUCHIDA MITSUO (right) TOLD NAGUMO, "I AM ready for the mission." The admiral said, "I have every confidence in you." And the attack commenced.

A message was drafted and sent to commanders in California, Panama, the Philippines and Hawaii: "The Japanese are presenting at 1 p.m. E.S.T. today what amounts to an ultimatum, also they are under orders to destroy their code machine immediately. Just what significance the hour set may have we do not know but be on alert accordingly."

By 12:01 p.m. on the East Coast—6:31 a.m. in Hawaii—the warning was filed at the War Department Signal Center for transmission to Panama, Manila and San Francisco. The War Department had been out of contact with Hawaii that morning and was attempting to relay the message to Honolulu. Teletype transmission to San Francisco was completed by 12:17 p.m. Washington time (6:47 a.m. in Hawaii). The warning was sent from San Francisco to RCA's Honolulu's cable office (an arm of the radio communications company), where it arrived at 7:33 a.m. Because that was too early for Teletype traffic to Fort Shafter, RCA sent the memo by messenger: a Japanese boy on a motorcycle. En route, the boy heard what sounded like gunfire.

Several minutes earlier, elsewhere on Oahu, two trainees had been preparing to close down the radar for daylight hours when they noticed blips on the screen—planes approaching at a range of 132 miles. Their lieutenant was not surprised; a flight of Fortresses from the West Coast was expected. Shut it down, he suggested, and go get some chow.

The strike force for Japan's Hawaiian Operation had begun to assemble at Hitokappu Bay in the Kuril Islands in November, while elsewhere, Japanese army and air corps units prepared to sweep other Pacific islands during, or right after, the assault on Pearl Harbor. By month's end, Japan wanted to lock up not only Indonesia but Guam, Midway and the Philippines. The success of the widespread operation depended on greatly disabling and

▲ **ZEROS WAITED ON THE CARRIER** *AKAGI*, **PRIOR TO DEPARTING for Pearl Harbor. A brilliantly engineered plane—superior to any U.S. fighter at the time—the Zero (known as a "Zeke") could also function as a bomber. Zeros were the planes that first launched the attack.**

"As the aircraft went off, they had their lights on, and it was like the sky was filled with fireflies."

ABE ZENJI

Dive Bomber Pilot, *Akagi*

"I was a squadron leader on the *Akagi*. Before I set off, I changed my old underwear to my new ones. I put on my best uniform, my flying uniform, the khaki-colored one. Every aircraft carrier had a shrine. I went underneath and prayed at the shrine. I bowed just once. 'I am going now,' I said.

When the first group left, before dawn, it was dark. As the aircraft went off, they had their lights on, and it was like the sky was filled with fireflies. It was a beautiful scene—183 aircraft in the dark sky.

It was getting brighter. I was at the back of the second fleet. There were 70 dive-bombers in the group. If you are flying, following another aircraft, the propeller engine makes a smoke stream, so to avoid it I was flying a little bit higher than the aircraft in front of me. I was near the end of the second group. The leader was at 3,000 meters. Each of the other planes was a little bit higher. I was at 3,500 meters. I felt like a shepherd watching the flock. I felt good about that.

I could see 200 to 300 bombs exploding on the ground. I immediately thought that the first group must be under counterattack from the Americans. From the sky, it was hard to distinguish the ships. I could see a huge ship, so I attacked. I learned later that it was the *Arizona*, already sinking. But it was my first mission; I just concentrated on what I was going to attack—I didn't think anything. There were lots of guns firing at me. I concentrated on my target.

I went to the *Arizona* Memorial recently and looked underneath. Every 40 seconds a bubble comes up. There are 1,177

dead buried there. I felt like those bubbles coming up were the bubbles of resentment of those dead. And I regret that. I shed a tear. Why Americans feel anger toward Japan—why they still hate us—I understand.

The most shameful thing is what I found out later. I found out that the Japanese government didn't declare war until after the attack."

IN 1991, 50 years after the attack, in an extraordinary public act of reconciliation, Abe appeared on the *Today Show*, live from Pearl Harbor, and shook hands with three American veterans of the attack. After that pivotal gesture, he devoted the rest of his life to being an emissary of peace and healing. On that day in 1941 he had dropped a 550-pound delayed fuse bomb onto the U.S.S. *Virginia*; it failed to detonate. A 19-year-old Marine bugler on board, Richard Fiske, had survived the war and, in 1991, had been a volunteer at the *Arizona* Memorial for nine years when he and Abe met. Against all odds, they became fast friends. Abe gave Fiske $300 and asked him to lay two roses on the Memorial each month and play taps. Fiske did so on the first Sunday of every month for 12 years until his death.

Abe was 21 when he graduated from Japan's Naval Academy in 1937. Pearl Harbor was his first attack mission. He continued flying throughout the war until stranded in the Mariana Islands in June 1944. After the war he was a colonel in the Japan Self-Defense Force. He died on April 6, 2007, at the age of 90.

thoroughly discouraging America's Pacific Fleet. That charge fell to Nagumo and his immense oceangoing force of six aircraft carriers, two battleships, three cruisers and nine destroyers.

That Nagumo's armada made its way undetected from Hitokappu Bay to within striking distance of Pearl Harbor borders on the miraculous. Maintaining strict radio silence for more than a week, the ships sailed north at approximately 43 degrees latitude, seeking less-traveled waters. They hit stormy seas. They plowed through fog. They made their way.

Three large submarines surged ahead as scouts. Twenty-seven other subs also traversed the ocean, their aim to surround Oahu and attack anything that attempted to escape the harbor. Five of these vessels bore midget submarines that would zip into Pearl Harbor before the attack began.

The strike force settled 230 miles north of Oahu, and from there, on December 7, 1941, at 6 a.m., the first wave of 183 planes—49 Kate bombers, each armed with one 1,760-pound armor-piercing bomb; 40 Kates carrying torpedoes; 51 Val dive bombers, each carrying a 551-pound bomb; and 43 Zero fighter planes—was launched from the carriers and roared toward Hawaii.

At 7:49 a.m., Air Group Commander Fuchida Mitsuo spotted Pearl Harbor: seven battleships in Battleship Row. At 7:53, he gave the signal by telegraph key: *to* and *ra*—or together, the word for "tiger." Over and over: *to-ra, to-ra, to-ra*.

The torpedo bombers dived to a level from which they would launch their weapons. Other bombers split off to hit Army and Navy airfields. The biggest planes flew steadily on, homing in on their targets. The Zeros, having swept down Oahu's west coast, prepared to strafe and bedevil. Their job as escorts was done, and they instantly shifted into gear as fighter planes.

Below, sailors were preparing for the 8 a.m. hoisting of the colors aboard the great ships. They saw the torpedo bombers screaming earthward. They saw the lethal shells in the water, incoming. A bomb exploded in the bay. The torpedoes sped toward the ships. At 7:58, the alarm went out: "Air raid, Pearl Harbor. This is not drill!" Within minutes the *West Virginia*, *Nevada*, *Oklahoma* and *California* had been struck by torpedoes. War was on.

◀ **A KATE, JAPAN'S PRINCIPAL TORPEDO BOMBER, LIFTED OFF** from the *Shokaku*, bound for Pearl. Owing to heavy seas, takeoffs were difficult from ships that were listing as much as 15 degrees, but there could be no delays that might snarl the complex strategy.

U.S.S. ARIZONA MEMORIAL/NPS

U.S. NAVY

The siege was swift and ruthless. Within moments a peaceful Sunday morning became an unimaginable nightmare. Soldiers and civilians, medics, clergy and children watched in horror as the Japanese torpedoes fell from the sky and exploded into the great ships. Children and wives were bundled up into the relative safety of the mountains, while their husbands and fathers rushed to duty, some of them never to be seen again. Hospital personnel were immediately inundated with the wounded and dying. Amid the chaos, noise and smoke, brave shipmen rushed to man their turrets, still blinking away the previous evening's merrymaking.

03:42 Ensign R.C. McCloy, aboard the minesweeper *Condor*, spots a periscope in the darkness.

03:57 The *Condor* sends a message to the destroyer *Ward*: "Sighted submerged submarine on westerly course, speed 9 knots."

06:00 The first wave of the Japanese attack takes off for Hawaii from ships anchored north of the islands.

06:26 Japanese pilots bound for Pearl Harbor see the sun rise, and the shafts of light bring to mind their naval flag.

06:45 After searching for hours, the *Ward* fires depth charges and sinks the Japanese sub.

(Previous Pages) **AUTUMN 1941: ALL IS QUIET ON THE WESTERN front. Note that this southwest orientation varies from the maps on the following pages.**

▲ **A VAL DIVE-BOMBER, HIT BY ANTIAIRCRAFT FIRE DURING THAT second wave, moments away from crashing.**

海軍省許可濟第七八三號

▲ **THIS PHOTO OF FORD ISLAND, FACING ROUGHLY EAST, WAS** taken from a Japanese plane minutes after the attack had begun. On the far side of the island, in Battleship Row, water and smoke gushed from the *West Virginia*, which had just been torpedoed, and from the *Oklahoma* (listing to port). On the near side (second and third from left), the light cruiser *Raleigh* and target ship *Utah* (mistaken for a battleship) had caught torpedoes. Two Kate torpedo bombers are visible, one over Battleship Row and the other over the Navy Yard, at right rear. This picture was seized after the war—note the Japanese writing at the bottom.

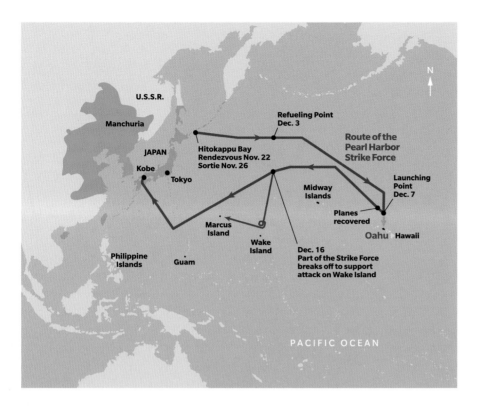

Route of the Pearl Harbor Strike Force

U.S.S.R.

Manchuria

JAPAN

Kobe

Tokyo

Hitokappu Bay
Rendezvous Nov. 22
Sortie Nov. 26

Refueling Point
Dec. 3

Launching
Point
Dec. 7

Midway
Islands

Planes
recovered

Oahu   Hawaii

Marcus
Island

Wake
Island

Dec. 16
Part of the Strike Force
breaks off to support
attack on Wake Island

Philippine
Islands

Guam

PACIFIC OCEAN

N

THESE THREE MAPS PROVIDE A TELESCOPED PORTRAIT OF THE ATTACK ON PEARL
Harbor. The overview above shows the route of the 31 Japanese ships, which included six
aircraft carriers, before and after the bombing. The small orange arrow indicates the 230-mile
journey that the planes took to reach Oahu. That island is represented in the map below; the
arrows indicate the primary flight paths of incoming Japanese aircraft. (Bombing, of course,
was not strictly confined to those paths.) The square at the bottom of the Oahu map
is magnified at right: Pearl Harbor as it existed at the moment of the attack.

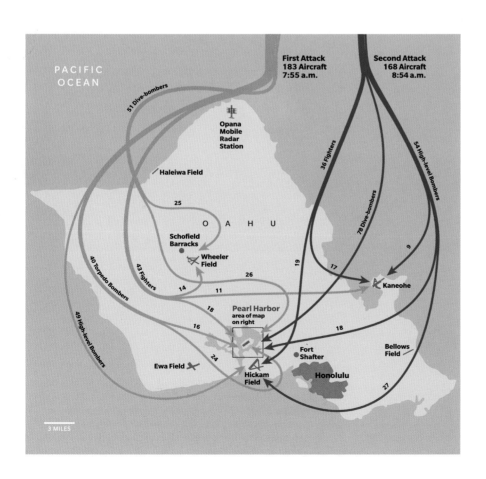

PACIFIC
OCEAN

First Attack
183 Aircraft
7:55 a.m.

Second Attack
168 Aircraft
8:54 a.m.

51 Dive-bombers

Opana
Mobile
Radar
Station

Haleiwa Field

36 Fighters

54 High-level Bombers

25

78 Dive-bombers

O A H U

Schofield
Barracks

Wheeler
Field

9

40 Torpedo Bombers

43 Fighters

19

17

14

11

26

Kaneohe

18

Pearl Harbor
area of map
on right

16

18

49 High-level Bombers

24

Ewa Field

Fort
Shafter

Bellows
Field

Hickam
Field

Honolulu

27

3 MILES

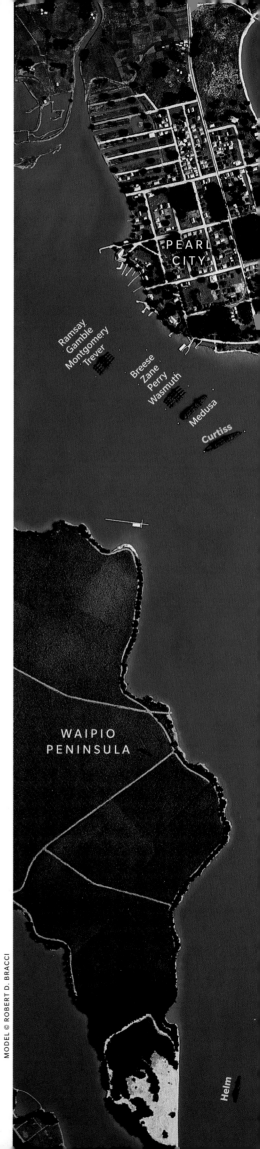

PEARL
CITY

Ramsay
Gamble
Montgomery
Trever

Breese
Zane
Perry
Wasmuth

Medusa

Curtiss

WAIPIO
PENINSULA

Helm

Monaghan
Farragut
Dale
Aylwin

Henley
Patterson
Ralph Talbot

Selfridge
Case
Tucker
Reid
Conyngham
Whitney

Blue

Phoenix

Phelps
MacDonough
Worden
Dewey
Hull
Dobbin

Solace

PEARL HARBOR
December 7, 1941

KEY TO SHIPS

Sunk
Heavy damage
Moderate damage
No damage

Utah
Raleigh
Detroit

Allen
Chew

Tangier

**FORD
ISLAND**

Nevada
Arizona
Tennessee
West Virginia **Vestal**
Maryland
Oklahoma
BATTLESHIP ROW

Pearl Harbor
Naval Air
Station

Neosho

California

**Seaplane
Base**

Avocet

Argonne
Sacramento

Ramapo
New Orleans
San Francisco
St. Louis
Honolulu

Pelias

Shaw

Downes
Cassein

Oglala
Helena
Pennsylvania

Cachalot

Bagley

**Submarine
Base**

**Hospital
Point**

Sumner
Castor

**Oil Storage
Tanks**

Navy Yard

**Cooling
Station**

**Oil Storage
Tanks**

Hickam Field

07:02 Privates Joseph Lockard and George Elliott pick up blips on radar. They are told by a superior that what they have spotted is an incoming flight of American planes.

07:49 Commander Fuchida Mitsuo, the head of the assault, issues the attack signal as his plane passes just off Lahilahi Point. Four minutes later he calls out, "Tora! Tora! Tora!"—code words confirming that the Japanese have surprised their enemy.

07:55 The raid begins at Pearl Harbor as the *Raleigh*, *Helena*, *Utah* and *Oklahoma* are struck. Years later, in an interview with Ronald E. Marcello of the University of North Texas Oral History Program, Seaman Garlen W. Eslick of the *Oklahoma* recalls, "This boy just slumped over. Blood was all over everything. I still didn't know what had happened ... I heard this thing roar over ... the officer-of-the-deck came on and announced, 'Man your battle stations.'"

07:56 There are two explosions on the *Arizona*. Pfc. James Cory: "The bridge shielded us from flames ... Around the edges in these open windows came the heat and the sensation of the blast. We cringed there ... I think that at this moment I wanted to flee, but this was impossible. You're on station, you're in combat."

07:58 As bombs explode on Ford Island, Lt. Comdr. Logan Ramsey hurries to the radio room and sends the message, "Air raid, Pearl Harbor. This is not drill!" Yeoman 1C. Leonard Webb rushes to get his wife and child to a car: "When we're almost to the car, my wife says, 'The baby doesn't have any diapers! Get some!' Bear in mind that this is Armageddon, and my wife has me chasing diapers!"

▲ **IT WAS ABOUT 8 A.M. IN THIS JAPANESE PHOTO, AND THE attack on Battleship Row was getting under way. (Note plane in circle.) Torpedoes can be seen streaking for the ships, which were, from left: the** *Nevada*, *Arizona* **(repair ship** *Vestal* **lay on outside),** *West Virginia* **outside of** *Tennessee*, **and** *Oklahoma* **outside of** *Maryland*. **The** *California* **(at far right),** *Oklahoma* **and** *West Virginia* **have been hit, as evidenced by ripples and spreading oil. The** *West Virginia* **was saved from capsizing when quick thinking by Lt. Claude V. Ricketts led to counterflooding measures that let the ship settle to the bottom on an even keel. The white smoke at rear issued from Hickam Field, the gray smoke from the light cruiser** *Helena*.

08:01 Ensign Joseph K. Taussig Jr. sounds the *Nevada*'s general quarters and rushes to his battle station. Injured as his ship is strafed, Taussig continues his work.

08:02 Twenty-five bombers dive toward Wheeler Field. "The sailor approximately six feet in front of me fell," says Pvt. Leslie Le Fan. "I stepped over him, and remember thinking to myself: 'That's the first dead man I have ever seen.'"

08:03 Machine and antiaircraft guns aboard the *Cummings*, *California*, *Swan* and the submarine *Cachalot* open fire.

08:06 A 1,763-lb. missile fired by PO Kanai Noboru hits the *Arizona*. It demolishes the forward magazine and kills nearly 1,000 men. "It was so vivid in my mind," says Private Le Fan, who saw the action from the Marine barracks. "[The *Arizona*] just quivered, buckled and then settled. It looked like … well, that killed it … It was so devastating."

08:06 The forward magazines of the *Arizona* were struck by a bomb, setting off shock waves that were felt by planes 10,000 feet above. In that instant, some 1,000 men perished, three of whom would receive the Medal of Honor. The *Arizona*, engulfed in furious flames and smoke in late morning, would burn for two days. The explosion caused the front upper portion of the ship to collapse into the hull; thus the forward superstructure tilted 45 degrees and forward guns hovered just above the waterline.

▲ **THE BURNING** *ARIZONA* **IS SHOWN IN A FRAME FROM A FILM SHOT** aboard the hospital ship *Solace*, which treated many of the *Arizona*'s casualties. (Right) Sailors on the stern of the *Tennessee* manned water hoses to keep burning oil away from their ship.

08:08 Two bombs strike the *West Virginia*, whose captain, Mervyn Bennion, is mortally wounded by a piece of shrapnel that flies over from the *Tennessee*. "A huge waterspout splashed over the stack of the ship and then tumbled down like an exhausted geyser," recalls Japanese commander Matsumura Midori, who fired one of the torpedoes that hit the ship. "What a magnificent sight." Webley Edwards at KGMB radio announces: "All Army, Navy and Marine personnel to report to duty." As Water Tender 2c. Emil T. Beran closes the hatch behind him on board the *Allen Chew*, he says, "God save us! This is the last time that I'm ever going to see the sunshine!" Beran will ultimately survive the attack.

08:10 (13:40 E.S.T.) In Washington, President Roosevelt is informed by Navy Secretary Frank Knox that there has been a sneak attack on Pearl Harbor. This is "just the kind of unexpected thing the Japanese would do," says FDR. "[A]t the very time they were discussing peace in the Pacific, they were plotting to overthrow it." Roosevelt remained calm, but he was already calculating the costs of war.

U.S. NAVY (2)

◀ **THE ATTACK WAS ONLY** minutes old, and the *Utah* already strained at her mooring ropes en route to capsizing. The *Utah* had been converted to a training and target ship, which was well known to Japanese airmen, whose instructions to ignore the vessel vanished in the heat of the moment.

▲ **IN THIS JAPANESE PHOTO,** the *Utah* (second from bottom) had gone belly-up. Other ships included, from top, the light cruisers *Detroit*, which was strafed but not damaged, and *Raleigh*, listing to port after a torpedo hit. The seaplane tender *Tangier* (bottom) suffered superficial damage from a near-miss bomb.

KERMIT TYLER

Lieutenant, Information Center

"**T**hey wanted me to come in [to the Information Center at Fort Shafter] on Sunday morning from 4:00 to 8:00. When I got there it was quiet.

A few plots showed up [on radar] starting about 6:15, which could very well have been Japanese scout planes. They came in and we plotted them, but there was no way of telling what they were. The problem was, we had no identification people on staff yet. A little after 7:00, one of the plotters came up to the balcony and started doing some work on a drafting board. He showed me that at 7:02 there was a plot at 132 miles and three degrees east of north. It made me think that it was probably B-17s.

At about 7:15 I got a call from Pvt. Joseph Lockard that he had the same plot. He said it was the biggest plot he had ever seen. Well, 12 B-17s could make a pretty big splash on his screen. I told him, 'Don't worry about it. It's O.K.' So that was the end of that. He hung up and I hung up.

After that, not a thing. A few minutes after 8:00 I stepped outside to take a breath of fresh air. I looked off to the west and saw puffs of smoke and a few planes. It looked like they were practicing dive-bombing. It turned out it was the attack. A few minutes later I had a call from a sergeant in operations at Wheeler Field that they had been attacked.

By that time they had the ships burning. We could see the carnage. You just felt like the world was ending. I had the distinct feeling that one of the bombs was going to land on this Information Center because it was such a well-planned attack and they hit everything at once. It was just unbelievable, overwhelming."

TYLER, with one day's experience at Fort Shafter's Information Center, was the only officer on duty the morning of December 7, 1941. After the war he continued his career in Utah and in England before retiring from the Air Force in 1961. He died on January 23, 2010, at the age of 96.

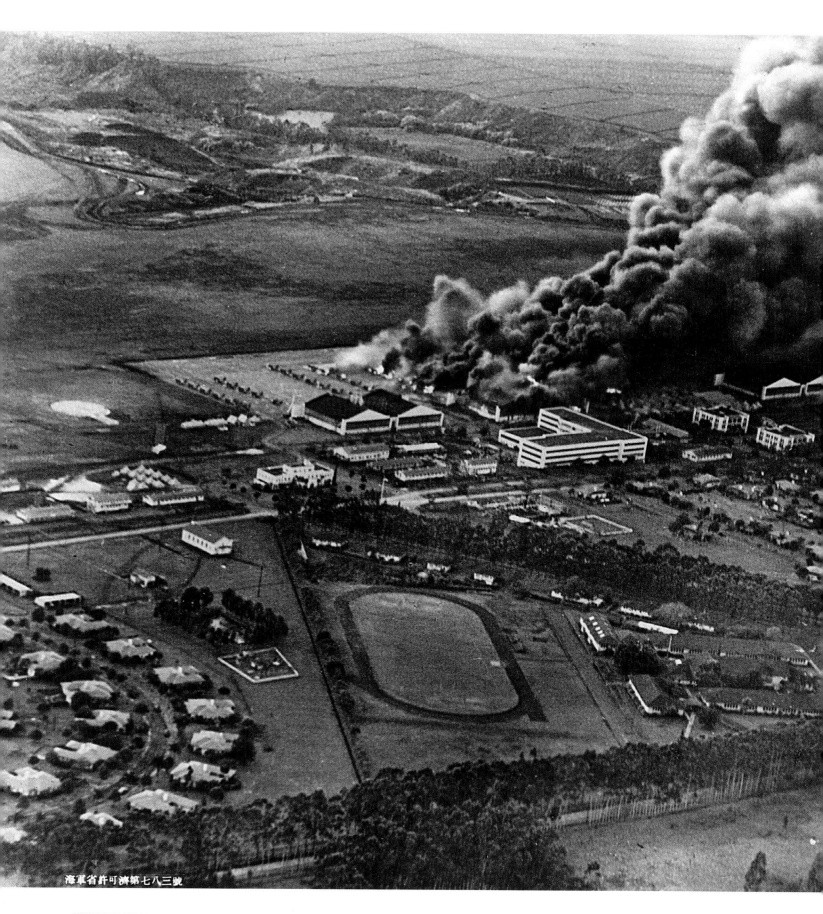

海軍省許可濟第七八三號

▲ WHEELER FIELD, THE ARMY AIR BASE IN CENTRAL OAHU, was under heavy attack in this Japanese photo taken during the first wave. Dive-bombers and Zeros laid waste to hangars, barracks and more than half of the 153 planes there. General Walter Short's preoccupation with sabotage led to planes being stored outside in plain sight—in neat rows perfect for the attackers. Only a handful of the 82 fighters got off the ground. In any case, many of them were obsolete and all of them had their ammo belts removed every night.

08:12 The *Utah* capsizes. "By the time I got to the door, the ship rolled over," says Seaman 2c. John Vaessen. "Well, I'm hanging on to everything—the door and anything I could grab—and the deck plates come flying at me, fire extinguishers—everything loose—and I was hit in many places but no sharp edges…I was just lucky that God was with me, that's for sure."

08:14 Americans set up machine guns at Wheeler Field and fire at Japanese planes, bringing down one Zero. "I helped to give the sacraments to the dying and aid to the suffering," says Father Marcus Valenta. "They had boys lying out on the lawn in front of a little first-aid station."

08:15 Rescue workers pull men out of the burning water. "Our own oil was bubbling up and congealing," says Pfc. James Cory of the *Arizona*. "People who have never seen this at sea cannot imagine what oil is like once it is exposed to cool seawater…It was catching fire slowly and was incinerating toward us."

08:17 The destroyer *Helm* clears the harbor, spots a Japanese submarine and fires on it—missing.

08:25 At Schofield Barracks, Lt. Stephen Saltzman and Sgt. Lowell Klatt grab rifles and fire at a Zero as it strafes them. The men keep shooting until the plane crashes.

08:25 Japanese planes attack Hawaiian firemen at Hickam Field, killing three. "They were so low you could see them grinning," says Machinist Mate 2c. Leon Bennett. "They were laughing, all smiles."

▶ **IN ONE OF THE FEW ACTION** pictures of personnel fighting back, three Marines at Ewa Field looked for a place from which to fire, while two others looked for something to fire at.

08:30 Sailors on the *Downes* open fire on attacking planes. "We had the .50-caliber machine guns," recalls Gunner's Mate 2c. Curtis Schulze. "They were water-cooled, and some of the men worried about the water, and I said, 'To hell with the damned water! Don't worry about it! Just start firing the goddamned things!'"

08:35 A number of U.S. planes returning from a scouting mission see that they cannot land on Ford Island. They head instead for Ewa Field to the west, where the Japanese have damaged or destroyed all 47 Marine planes. When one of the planes touches the ground, a Marine runs out and shouts, "For God's sake, get into the air or they'll strafe you too!" The plane manages to take off again.

08:35 The first wave of the attack ends. "Amputees. They started coming in, and they had arms and legs just shot off—a terrible mass of tissues, bones, blood," recalls 2d Lt. Elizabeth Murphy, a nurse at Tripler General Hospital. "Oh, heavens! I had never seen anything like this!"

▶ **THE JAPANESE VAL** dive-bombers at right were photographed from one of a dozen B-17s bound for the Philippines, with a scheduled first stop at Hickam Field. They arrived in the middle of the fracas, but had set out without ammo to save fuel for the long trip from California.

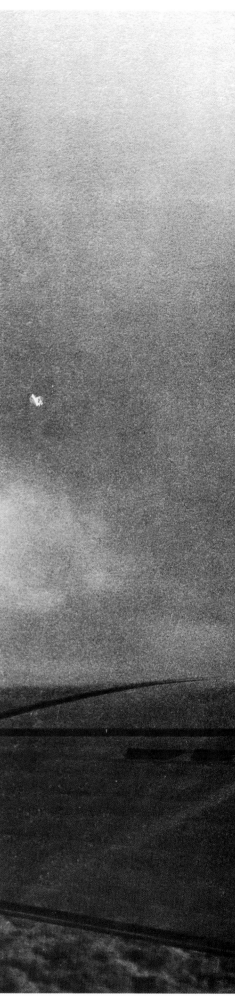

▲ **ALL THE PLANES LANDED SAFELY EXCEPT CAPT. RAYMOND** Swenson's, which broke in two as it crash-landed after a Japanese shell set off magnesium flares in the radio compartment. This was the expected group of B-17s that had led to the squelching of earlier radar reports of incoming aircraft.

(Following Pages) **PEARL HARBOR, 9 A.M. THE SECOND ATTACK WAS** at full throttle, but by now American defenses had awakened and were sending up this mass of antiaircraft fire. The photo was taken from the hills northwest of the harbor. A huge, billowing column of smoke spewed from the stricken *Arizona*. The smoke left of the *Arizona* came from the destroyers *Shaw*, *Cassin* and *Downes*, which were in dry dock at the Navy Yard.

U.S.S. ARIZONA MEMORIAL/NPS

U.S.S. ARIZONA MEMORIAL/NPS

08:47 The destroyer *Blue* gets under way, with Ens. Nathan F. Asher at the helm. When two planes dive toward the ship, sailors respond with .50-caliber machine guns. (Asher later says he had no idea how the men "got their ammunition from the magazines to the guns in the fast and swift manner that they did.") After they down a Japanese plane, crewmen on the Blue stop shooting and pat one another on the back.

08:50 The battleship *Nevada* heads out, in part because the wounded Ensign Taussig has managed to start the second boiler. The Japanese spot the ship leaving the harbor and determine to sink her, hoping to block the channel. "The Japanese bombers swarmed down on us like bees," recalls Lt. Lawrence Ruff.

08:50 (14:20 E.S.T.) In Washington, Secretary of State Cordell Hull, well aware of what is transpiring in Hawaii, erupts when given a note from the Japanese breaking off peace talks: "I have never seen a document that was more crowded with infamous falsehoods and distortions—on a scale so huge that I never imagined until today that any government on this planet was capable of uttering them."

◀ **AT APPROXIMATELY THE time of the second wave,** sailors in all manner of dress at the Naval Air Station on Ford Island reloaded ammunition clips and belts—and kept an eye out for the new enemy.

08:54 The second wave of the Japanese attack, this one under the command of Lt. Comdr. Shimazaki Shigekazu, swarms over Pearl. Fifty-four high-level bombers and 78 dive-bombers spread out to hit ships, airfields and barracks throughout Oahu, while 36 fighters maintain air control.

09:00 A formation of Zeros strikes Bellows Field, blowing up a gasoline truck and hitting a plane from the 44th squadron as it tries to take off. Just in case anyone on the island remains unconvinced, KGMB radio's Edwards blurts over the air, "This is the real McCoy!"

09:05 At Wheeler Field, 27 Japanese planes attack aircraft that are parked on the ground. The Japanese also strike barracks, service buildings and a baseball field.

09:06 A bomb hits the *Downes* while she sits in dry dock. Another strikes Adm. Husband E. Kimmel's flagship, the *Pennsylvania*, detonating guns and ammunition.

09:07 An order is issued instructing Americans to cease firing on U.S. B-17s attempting to land at Hickam Field.

U.S. NAVY

NATIONAL ARCHIVES

◀ **BLASTED DURING THE FIRST** wave and threatened by fiery oil spilling from the *Arizona*, the *Nevada* made for the open seas at about 9 a.m.

▲ **THIS WAS THE VIEW FROM PIER ONE OF THE SUBMARINE**
Base, looking toward the Navy Yard, at about 9:15 a.m. Sailors in the
foreground, with rifles and pistol belts, crouched as they searched
for enemy aircraft. To their left was the sub *Narwhal* and at far left,
the *Dolphin*. Coming from the right was the oiler *Neosho*, which had
escaped from Battleship Row with her perilous cargo of aviation fuel.

◀ OF THE MANY INSTANCES of bravery at Pearl, one of the most visible was the *Nevada*'s attempt to sortie, or depart from the harbor. The sight of the gallant ship electrified and emboldened Americans on the shore. Minutes later, under withering fire, the ship beached itself rather than bottle up the harbor.

▼ SAILORS MANNED THE guns on the seaplane tender *Avocet* in the foreground, while the *Nevada* (center), her bow in flames, had been swung around by harbor currents.

"I went up a couple of decks and smelled fresh air. That was the most magnificent breath of air I ever took."

CHARLES MERDINGER
Ensign, U.S.S. *Nevada*

"I was ashore that Saturday and got this little tree. It was going to brighten up our little cabin for Christmas. On Sunday, all of a sudden I heard general quarters and the bugle. I got out of my pajamas and got through my second sock when a fellow ran by my room and yelled, 'It's the real thing.' There was a huge explosion and machine-gun fire. I went right to my battle station, which was further down. I ran the range keeper, which calculated how the big guns should be trained and fired. Since we were not going to shoot 14-inch guns at planes, our station became a sort of central communications area.

There had been so many people wounded up above on the five-inch guns that they needed relief. I was told to send half of the men immediately. I just looked around and figured out which were the least important phone lines being manned. I picked those people and told them to go. It was 'Aye, aye, sir.' Nobody wanted to take a vote or discuss the matter or philosophize about it.

Soon after the attack, the *Nevada* got under way. Then the Japs really jumped us. They must have hit us a couple of times in the course of that run in the channel. The ship was beginning to tilt, going down. We were ordered to beach the ship to keep the channel clear. The ship settled down and the main deck almost was awash, a foot or two from the surface.

Our room was relatively calm and quiet. There was no sense of panic. When the main power went out, I told everyone to lie down on the deck to conserve air. Most of us removed our shirts or opened them because it was kind of hot. We didn't really have any change of air down there.

Late in the day, water began to drip from overhead. That was the first inkling we had that we were basically in an air bubble. Then the gaskets on the door by which we entered started to give way, and the water started coming in. It was a couple of inches, up around our ankles. It never occurred to me at the time how we were going to get out. When the water came in the door, I realized that we were really in for it. I called up the executive officer and requested permission to secure. He said, 'Permission granted.' I told everybody we were going to secure. There was no mad rush. I opened the other door to the next room, and everybody filed out. We had been in there from eight in the morning till about three in the afternoon.

I recall bodies lying around in the other room, and it being smoky. I went up a couple of decks and smelled fresh air. That was the most magnificent breath of air I ever took. When I got out and looked around, the whole world was on fire. Ships were burning and oil on the water was on fire. My first reaction was 'Lord, thanks that I made it out in one piece.'"

MERDINGER served on the *Alabama* during the war; afterward he won a Rhodes Scholarship and earned a doctorate from Oxford. He became president of Washington College and deputy director of Scripps Oceanography. He died on December 13, 2013, at the age of 95.

09:08 Dive-bombers attack the *Raleigh*; one bomb misses the ship's aviation tanks by mere feet. "A lot of times planes were coming at us from all angles," remembers Seaman 1c. Nick L. Kouretas, a gunner. "I'd try to concentrate on one target. They'd say: 'Get this guy!' you know, and I'd lead him, hoping I could get him. I know I was scared as hell."

09:10 In order not to block the channel that leads out of the harbor, Lt. Comdr. J.F. Thomas beaches the wounded *Nevada* at Hospital Point.

09:15 Captain J.W. Bunkley, who has spent the night ashore, returns to the *California*. The ship has been hit numerous times and is in flames. "If we had had a 15-minute warning, we could have been partially prepared to defend ourselves," says Seaman Jerod Haynes. "Anything would have beaten [being] a sittin' duck." Within an hour, Bunkley is forced to abandon his ship.

09:20 A bomb passes through the dock alongside the cruiser *Honolulu*. It explodes underwater, flooding part of the ship and damaging her oil tanks.

▶ **THE FORWARD MAGAZINES** of the destroyer *Shaw* took a direct hit as she lay in floating dry dock. The impact of three 550-pound bombs tore off the entire bow of the ship. The explosives might have been meant for the *Nevada* (gun turrets visible at lower right), already beached for 20 minutes.

NATIONAL ARCHIVES

U.S. NAVY

▲ **THIS PICTURE WAS TAKEN ONLY SECONDS LATER FROM AN** air base on Ford Island, where sailors, standing amid a squadron of wrecked planes, watched the fireball from the *Shaw* ascend.

WARREN K. TAYLOR
Ensign, U.S.S. *Sumner*

"I was an ensign on the *Sumner*, a survey ship. We were at the Submarine Base, at a dock in front of the administration building. The first thing that we knew, the officer of the deck said there were planes dropping bombs. I ran up onto the fantail. The torpedo planes were coming down East Loch, which was perpendicular to Battleship Row. They needed the long approach to drop their torpedoes. They were flying slowly, and lowly.

If this was a drill, it was a hell of a drill. A little bit later, the first message we received was, 'This is not a drill.'

The first thing I saw was a torpedo plane, which had a red sun and corps insignia. They were paying no attention to us, but they must have been only 100 or 200 yards from us, very close. I had been in the Navy only six weeks— I thought this was a game, the reds against the blues.

General quarters was sounded. I went to my station. I was a supply officer and could type, so I was at a coding board. My job was coding and decoding messages— cryptography. From my post I could see things exploding.

We had primitive antiaircraft guns on the *Sumner*, old-fashioned and ineffective. But one of the guns on the fantail shot down one of the torpedo planes. It was only about 8:00 or 8:05. We almost got another. The gun was just in front of me. The shell missed by three or four feet. A communications officer later told me that we were given credit for being the first ship to shoot down a Japanese plane, although a shore battery did receive credit for having shot one down earlier.

We weren't far from the dry dock where the *Pennsylvania* was. The destroyers *Cassin* and *Downes* had been hit. Their seams were opened up, oil was spilling out, and the oil was on fire. The shells were pirouetting through the air. It was spectacular, like the Fourth of July.

It was all over very quickly."

TAYLOR served in the Navy until December 1945. He served as a California Superior Court judge and lived in Davis, California. He died on December 6, 2015, at the age of 95.

U.S. NAVY

▲ **NOT EVERY SHIP AT PEARL** Harbor was damaged in the attack. In this picture, taken at 9:26 from a moving car north of the harbor, there are two groups of destroyers and their tenders, all of which survived without harm.

09:28 Gunners aboard the *Mugford* shoot down a Japanese bomber after it pulls out of its dive alongside the ship's port bow.

09:30 In the ships' logs of the *Antares* and *Whitney*, it is noted that the attack may be over. Years later, Seaman Eslick tells the Oral History Program what it was like to be trapped aboard the *Oklahoma*: "You did a little praying and thinking things. You think about your family. I had a younger sister who was just a baby. I thought about my brothers and all my family. Would I ever see them again? But I never once...thought that I was going to die...I

knew I was in one heck of a predicament...I was hoping I would get out. I knew what kind of situation I was in, and I came to the conclusion of what I was up against...With all these fumes and stuff, my eyes were burning. I had saltwater, gasoline, bunker oil and stuff all in my eyes; and I'd swallowed I don't know how much saltwater...We stayed in that compartment rapping out this SOS. I don't know how long it was. We could hear the boys, some of them, in this one compartment next to us, and they were hollering for help for a good long time. There wasn't anything we could do about it, and then they became quiet. They evidently drowned."

NATIONAL ARCHIVES

U.S. NAVY

09:37 A large explosion on the battleship *Cassin* causes her to roll over onto the *Downes*.

09:40 The flames on the *West Virginia* reach as high as the foretop. Wounded are being removed from the ship.

09:41 "It was noted by everyone participating in action that after an hour or more heavy thirst was experienced requiring considerable drinking water," notes the ship's log of the *Pennsylvania*. "This confirms the necessity of having water at all battle stations."

09:43 Sailors aboard the *Tern* pull survivors out of the water. They will rescue 47 in all.

09:50 The *Blue* picks up the signal of a submarine. She maneuvers to attack and then drops six depth charges. An oil slick and air bubbles rise to the surface. The ship then detects another signal from a submarine that appears to be bearing down on the *St. Louis*. That sub, too, is sunk by a depth charge.

10:00 The Japanese first wave returns, victorious and exultant, to its aircraft carriers north of Hawaii.

▲ **THE SEAPLANE BASE ON THE SOUTHWEST POINT OF FORD**
Island was one of the earliest targets. This picture of Seaplane Hangar No. 6 may have been taken during the second wave. At lower left, men with rifles scanned the skies.

◀ **AT KANEOHE NAVAL AIR STATION, A SAILOR SPRINTED PAST**
burning PBY patrol planes. Kaneohe was strafed in the first wave, then hit with high-level bombing. Later strafing finished the job. The toll was fearsome: Of the 36 planes stationed there, 30 were destroyed. The only three that survived intact were in the air at the time of the assault.

NATIONAL ARCHIVES

◄ **FROM ON HIGH, A BOMBER SAVORED THE VIEW DURING THE** second wave. In the foreground is Hickam Field, which has been pounded. The black smoke at right center rose from Battleship Row, where the capsized *Oklahoma* is visible. The listing *California* is at left, and the black smoke to her left issued from the *Shaw*. Below Battleship Row, the oiler *Neosho* steamed toward the Submarine Base.

10:00 Robert Shivers, head of the FBI's Honolulu bureau, places a guard at the Japanese consulate. Elsewhere, wounded are being attended to, dead are being found. Seaman 1c. Nick L. Kouretas of the *Raleigh* is looking frantically for his brother: "Every time we brought a load over to the landing, I would jump off and run up the landing, because they were laying them like cordwood, a body here and a body there, with a walkway down the center where they would try to identify them by their dog tags, with their heads pointing into the walkway. I would run along the aisle and, knowing my brother's characteristics, look for him. He chewed his nails. I knew where he had a wart; I knew every little mark on his body. I would get so far, and I'd say, 'Well, this guy looks like him,' but I couldn't see his face. I'd pick up a hand, and I'd say, 'No, that's not him,' and then go on." Seaman Kouretas's brother survived the attack.

10:04 A Japanese midget sub shoots two torpedoes at the *St. Louis*, which has made its way clear of the channel. Captain George Rood reacts and has the ship change course; the torpedoes strike near the harbor's entrance. Sailors fire at the sub when it surfaces.

(Following Pages) **BLACK, OILY SMOKE FROM THE CARNAGE** of Battleship Row provided this nightmarish backdrop to the Marine Barracks Parade Grounds at the Navy Yard. The Marine in the foreground seemed to register an appropriate disbelief as his comrades awaited another attack. Yeoman 1c. Leonard Webb was there: "We were . . . trying to load clips with seven thumbs on each hand. And here comes a Jap Zero . . . We didn't only flatten out. We went grass roots. I'm sure we got down to the roots."

VICTOR DELANO

Ensign, U.S.S. *West Virginia*

"The torpedoes demolished the whole side of the ship. We could hear the people on the other side of the watertight bulkheads. They were screaming. There was nothing that we could do.

By the time I got topside, the whole port side of the ship was smashed in. There were fires. The *West Virginia* for a long time had bragged about being the smartest battleship in the fleet. Now here was the ship just completely in shambles.

Captain Bennion had just been severely wounded—hit by shrapnel that had ripped his whole interior. I was told to do whatever I could for him. I got him to a better spot. I got a first-aid kit. They were supposed to have morphine in it, but that was a drug and we weren't at war, so they hadn't authorized the morphine. I soaked a cloth in ether and tried to make him more comfortable.

Then Lieutenant Ricketts arrived. He was the one who saved the ship from rolling over. He went below and counter-flooded. If he hadn't done that, we could have rolled over just the way the *Oklahoma* did.

I remember seeing the second wave. I must have been up there when the *Arizona* blew up. I saw other harbor activity. I saw the *Nevada* get under way and go by, and it got attacked and went aground.

I got two machine guns operating. An officer and two enlisted men arrived, and I assigned them to these guns and showed them how to operate them. The second wave was mainly horizontal bombers, up too high to be bothered by any .50-caliber machine guns. But the gunners didn't know that. They were feeling pretty deadly about this thing."

DELANO was the son of a Navy captain and a distant cousin of President Franklin D. Roosevelt. He died on August 8, 2014, at the age of 94, and is buried at Arlington National Cemetery.

U.S. NAVY

▲ **TWO BATTLESHIPS UNDER siege:** The *West Virginia* (center, foreground), shredded by bombs and torpedoes, was on fire and sinking. Behind her, the *Tennessee* was struck by two bombs but would emerge from repairs in May 1943 and go on to participate in some of the most critical actions in the war, from Tarawa to Okinawa. At far left, the hull of the *Oklahoma* is visible behind rescue boats.

10:05 Hawaii's Governor Joseph Poindexter calls local newspapers to announce a state of emergency for the entire territory.

10:10 As an uneasy sense that the air attack has ended spreads throughout Oahu, ships report and mobilize—even as sailors keep watch for a third wave of planes. The *Reid* reports that it has suffered no damage or casualties, and gets under way.

10:20 Rumors are everywhere. A U.S. attack group of 15 VSBs, each carrying half-ton bombs, is sent to scout 30 miles south of Pearl, as there have been reports of enemy carriers and possible landing forces.

10:23 The *Wasmuth* drops one depth charge. There are no signs that it hits any subs.

10:30 To the west, at Japanese Imperial headquarters in Tokyo, it is announced that Japan is now at war with the United States of America.

10:36 The *Wasmuth* drops another depth charge, and this time a spread of oil and bubbles indicates a hit.

11:27 Four A-20s join the search for enemy vessels reported to the south. The knowledge that Pearl Harbor is still vulnerable weighs heavily on the pilots. However, the feared third wave of attack never appears.

◄ **SAILORS ON THE ROOF OF THE NAVAL AIR STATION** headquarters witnessed the awesome spectacle of a 32,000-ton battleship in dire straits. The flagship *California* was hit very early by two torpedoes and was later struck by a bomb. Still, she was nearly ready to get under way when boiling oil, drifting down Battleship Row, placed the ship in urgent danger. This picture was taken at 10:02, as the *California*'s crew followed orders to abandon ship. By the time she could be reboarded, it was too late to control flooding wrought by the torpedo warheads.

11:35 The *Breese* picks up the sound of a submarine and drops two depth charges. Soon after, an oil slick appears, followed by debris. The *Breese* continues the attack by dropping four more depth charges. Destroyers in the area hurry to the scene to make certain that the sub has been destroyed. Even as most of the Japanese air strike force is safe on carriers many miles to the north, ready to head for home, Japanese submariners remain vulnerable in Pearl Harbor.

11:42 Believing that the Japanese have used—and perhaps are still using—radio signals to home in on the area, the U.S. Army orders all local stations off the air. Only special announcements may be aired.

11:46 Japanese troops are again reported to be landing on Oahu—another of many false sightings.

12:10 Pilots led by Lt. Comdr. Halstead Hopping set out for an area 200 miles north of Hawaii, searching for the Japanese.

12:21 It is reported that there are nine unidentified aircraft over Guam. The Japanese do, in fact, attack that island on December 7.

12:30 Honolulu police raid the Japanese embassy. They find consulate members burning coded books in a washtub. The police also seize a large envelope filled with undestroyed papers. At this point, all is still confusion, and there is no telling what might be invaluable or incriminating.

13:00 Commander Fuchida lands aboard the *Akagi*. His is the last plane to return to the Japanese carriers.

U.S. NAVY

◀ **IN THE BOWELS OF HELL: THE *CALIFORNIA* WAS CONCEALED** in the ferocious black smoke at left. The battleship visible at center is the *Maryland*. In the cruel tapestry of smoke behind her, the lighter color likely issued from the *Arizona*, and the darker plume at center was mainly from the *West Virginia*. To the right of that can be seen the white hull of the capsized *Oklahoma*. On the far right, beyond the cement mooring quay, a harbor tug directed a spout of water toward the inferno. To the left of the tug, small rescue craft braved the burning oil in search of survivors.

13:12 The U.S. Army reports that four enemy transports are off Barbers Point to the southwest of Pearl Harbor, thus continuing the day's stream of erroneous intelligence.

13:30 Hawaii's territorial director of civil defense orders nighttime blackouts. Meanwhile, many miles to the north, signal flags are waved aboard the Japanese aircraft carrier *Akagi*, setting in motion the fleet's withdrawal from the region.

15:00 Officers aboard the *Tennessee* pick up a report that Wake Island has been attacked by as many as 30 Japanese bombers.

16:25 Governor Poindexter institutes martial law on all Hawaiian islands.

16:28 As search and rescue efforts continue throughout the harbor, the fire on the *West Virginia* is reported to be finally under control.

21:00 U.S. bombers arriving at Oahu from the aircraft carrier *Enterprise*—which has been on maneuvers away from Pearl Harbor, and which will subsequently play a crucial and heroic role in the Pacific war—are mistaken by American ground troops for enemy planes, and are fired upon. "You could have read a newspaper by the tracer bullets," remembers Seaman Virgle Wilkerson.

21:14 A report from the stores-and-supply ship *Antares* says that the glare in Pearl Harbor is getting brighter as fires grow in intensity.

▶ **THIS VIEW LOOKS DOWN PIER 1010 TOWARD THE NAVY YARD'S** dry docks. In the foreground, the ancient minelayer *Oglala* lay on her side after being smashed by adjacent explosions on the cruiser *Helena*, here moored to *Oglala*'s left. The *Oglala* had occupied the usual berth of the battleship *Pennsylvania*, whose mast is visible beyond the *Helena* and in front of smoke from the burning destroyers *Cassin* and *Downes*. The billowing smoke at right came from the *Shaw*, whose stern is visible in the floating dry dock. On the far right is the *Nevada*, beached and aflame.

05:15 (DECEMBER 8, MORNING) Hawaiian police erroneously report enemy parachute troops landing in Kaliki Valley. "We each had our rifles loaded," says Private Le Fan, who the day before had seen a man cut down right in front of him at Wheeler Field. "We had our pistols loaded, and we were given orders to shoot anything that moved."

05:17 Submarines are sighted off Diamond Head. "A thing that kept going through my mind was: 'Oh, hell! They are going to land!'" says Machinist Mate 2c. Leon Bennett of the *Neosho*. "There was no way we could have kept a landing force from invading... [N]ot only the Navy but the Army and Marines were all totally disorganized."

06:45 Police radio reports that all schools are closed, and urges citizens to stay home. Years later, Dan Wentrcek, who was a fireman third class on the *Nevada*, recalls the atmosphere of December 8 in an interview with the University of North Texas Pearl Harbor Oral History Program: "We went back out the next day and tried to clean up... They took a group of us for burial detail on Aiea Landing. We worked over there as they would pick up bodies... They'd find them floating out in the water, and they'd bring them over, or the pieces, and then they had pharmacist's mates over there who would take fingerprints if they were unidentifiable... [T]hey brought the bodies in, and we had a bunch of pine boxes there that'd been made up... If they needed some help, why, we'd help them put a body in a box, and they would give it a number. A lot of times they had a bunch of pieces. We'd just have to put them in a box."

"The casualties, I am sorry to say, were extremely heavy."
— FRANKLIN DELANO ROOSEVELT

(Previous Page) **FOLLOWING AN ANCIENT HAWAIIAN TRADITION,** American sailors placed leis on the grave sites of their fallen comrades not far from the Kaneohe Naval Air Station. Graves were dug along the shore of the Pacific Ocean. Many soldiers were burying the very men they had served beside.

▲ **AN AERIAL VIEW OF THE DAMAGE DONE IN BATTLESHIP ROW.** The *Arizona* is at the bottom, and ahead of her the sunken *West Virginia* was outside the *Tennessee*. Ahead of the *Tennessee* was the *Maryland*, and outside of her rested the capsized *Oklahoma*. In the upper-left corner, the *California*, sunk, was surrounded by vessels.

I n the aftermath of the attack, Marines and sailors, surrounded by wreckage, scoured the sky for signs of the enemy. Reconnaissance planes took stock of the damage. Battleship Row lay in ruin. The *Cassin* had been slammed over onto the *Downes*. (Both destroyers would be rebuilt but required new hulls). The *Arizona* and the sunken *West Virginia* were more damaged than the *Tennessee*. To free the "Big Tenn," the Navy Yard had to dynamite her forward quay. Ahead of the *Tennessee* was the *Maryland*, and next to her rested the capsized *Oklahoma*, with a barge alongside to assist ongoing rescue efforts. The *California* had sunk and was surrounded by smaller vessels. The *Pennsylvania* had sustained relatively light damage despite being a sitting duck.

Dry dock activity in the Navy Yard was at a fever pitch. The *Shaw* had her bow blown off and lay at an angle in the floating dry dock. The torpedoed *Helena* was in for repairs. A crane still stood amid the damage done by the enemy fire. It had been operated by civilian yard worker George Walters, who had moved the device back and forth during the attack in an effort to divert low-flying planes from the battleships. Dark oil streaks could be seen all through the harbor.

▼ **THIS VIEW OF THE NAVY YARD SHOWS DRY DOCK ACTIVITY.**
At the top lay the *Shaw*; beneath her the torpedoed *Helena* was in for repairs. Below the *Helena* was the *Pennsylvania*, and to her left the wrecked destroyers *Downes* and *Cassin*. The *Pennsylvania* was actually in dry dock at the time of the attack and sustained only minor damage.

(Following Pages) **AT THE SOUTH END OF THE SEAPLANE BASE PBY** ramp on Ford Island, Marines and sailors scoured the afternoon sky for signs of the enemy. They were surrounded by sandbags and parts of wrecked PBYs. In the background, the *Nevada* is beached at Waipio Point; tugs had taken her there after she ran aground at Hospital Point.

The island of Oahu was filled with death and destruction on that fateful day. Just as all soldiers know that they may have to make the ultimate sacrifice, so is it true that in every war, civilians, too, will perish. Honolulu, just a few miles from Pearl Harbor, was clobbered by antiaircraft shells from American guns that had missed their mark. Ordinarily, time fuses on the shells made them burst in the air; in the chaos of the attack, many fuses weren't set, and the shells detonated when they hit the ground. There were explosions all over the city.

Makeshift aid stations were quickly set up all around the island. Losses sustained during the attack were stunning: 2,403 Americans were killed, another 1,178 wounded. Eighteen ships were sunk or seriously damaged, while 347 planes were destroyed or damaged. Had Nagumo not ordered the Japanese ships to turn back before the third

U.S. NAVY (2)

◀ **THE CARCASS OF THE** *Arizona* **in Battleship Row. It was hit four times by Japanese bombers. Of the more than 2,400 people that died at Pearl Harbor and 1,000 injured, almost half the casualties were from the** *Arizona*. **Today, the wreck is considered a "war grave" and continues to leak oil 75 years after its demise.**

▼ **A BARGE HELPED WITH** rescue work at the capsized *Oklahoma*. **The battleship had been hit by 9 torpedoes, eventually sinking and taking 430 lives with her. The damage was too extensive to salvage the great battleship. It was hauled to dry dock, stripped of its guns and essential parts and decommissioned in 1944.**

KAY AND FRANK TREMAINE
Civilians

Frank: We arrived in Honolulu in June of 1940 when the United Press news service transferred me there to run its two-man bureau. The military was already getting quite active in Hawaii. It was bustling.

Kay: The night of December 6, we went to a black-tie dinner dance at the Fort DeRussey Officer's Club on Waikiki Beach. Before going home, four of us walked outside. It was a balmy night. There were these heat flashes. It looked like shelling was going on. Commander [George] Gelley made the prophetic remark, "Just like the calm before the storm."

Frank: Early in the morning I was awakened by antiaircraft firing, growing and growing in intensity. When I got to the windows I could see puffs in the air out toward Pearl. On a hunch I called the Army headquarters at Fort Shafter. A friend of mine, Harry Albright, was the press officer. I said, "Harry, you know what is going on?" He said, "You can say we are under attack." I said, "Who is it, Harry? You don't think it is the Germans, do you?" Kay turned on the radio. A friend of ours named Webley Edwards was on the air saying, "This is an air raid, this is no drill. Take cover." I got on the phone. As soon as I sent as many messages as I could, reporting what I had seen and what I had found out, I threw on some clothes. Off I went.

Kay: A crowd had gathered around the swimming pool and was looking out toward Pearl. I heard that siren sound of a falling bomb that they always used in the movies. It hit the side of the hill, and a fragment grazed the forehead of a man standing by the pool. It was one of our own antiaircraft shells.

Frank: I tried to get to Pearl. Traffic was a horrible mess. I got out of line and drove down the other side of the highway,

hoping I didn't meet anybody coming in the other direction. Hickam Field is right next to Pearl Harbor. I could see barracks that had taken a lot of hits. There was extensive damage to aircraft along the edge of the field. There were wounded. I phoned three or four times to the bureau to report what I was seeing. A little bit after 11, I was on my fourth call and was told, "You might as well hold it now. The Navy has cut off all communications." By the time I got into town it was all pretty quiet.

Kay: There were rumors all day saying that Japanese were landing in the hills above us. All kinds of things, all false. One of the smartest things I did was make a big batch of eggnog. The egg and the milk settled our stomachs, and the alcohol settled our nerves—we didn't know if the attack was coming back or not. You don't realize how quickly the sun goes down out there, and all of a sudden we were caught by darkness. We didn't dare even light a flame on the stove to cook. Here we were just a target right on top of this hill. But nothing came.

Frank: Far as I know, I was the first newsman to see what had happened. I never thought of Pearl in terms of history-making, not until a long time later. As life goes on and people ask me about these things, I sort of step away and see it more as a historic event than a big exciting day in our lives.

THE TREMAINES spent the duration of the war working throughout the Pacific. Frank remained with a news bureau, while Kay worked for the Army as a cryptographer and then for the *Advertiser* as a journalist. Frank died at the age of 92 on the sixty-fifth anniversary of Pearl Harbor: December 7, 2006. Kay still lives in Georgia.

◄ **TWENTY-ONE SHIPS IN** the harbor were destroyed by the Japanese attack on Pearl Harbor. Despite the carnage the Pacific Fleet was rebuilt, with all but three ships returning to duty to contribute to the Allies' victory four years later.

wave, these numbers would have been considerably higher. The U.S. forces suffered staggering losses, but when they fought back, it was with a vengeance. Perhaps the spirit of the day—and of the long years to come—was best exemplified by Navy Chaplain Howell Forgy on the cruiser *New Orleans* when he exhorted the men, "Praise the Lord and pass the ammunition!" Twenty-nine Japanese planes were shot from the skies that day.

By early evening on December 7, several hundred men, women and children had gathered outside the White House in Washington, D.C., awaiting word, keeping vigil, seeking some kind of communion. Inside, the president was dictating a draft of the message he would deliver to Congress asking for a declaration of war. After a quiet dinner in his study, he went, at 8:30, to the Oval Office to brief his cabinet. There, he was blunt: "The casualties, I am sorry to say, were extremely heavy."

▲ **TWENTY-NINE JAPANESE** planes were shot from the skies, including this dive-bomber from the carrier *Kaga*, which had been piloted by Lt. Suzuki Mimori.

In the days after, grim discoveries were made everywhere in and around Pearl Harbor, while clues to what had happened were sought behind closed doors. Sailors trapped in the hulls of ships, some of them ill from having lain in pools of oil and water, were rescued. Bodies washed ashore. Death notices in the form of telegrams were frantically assembled. Dispatched under the authority of the Secretary of War or of the Navy, the wires were sent to next of kin as soon as possible so that the terrible news wouldn't arrive first by radio or newspaper. Wesley and Edward Heidt were among three dozen pairs of brothers on the U.S.S. *Arizona*. Not a single pair survived intact. Meanwhile, on December 11, Secretary of State Knox arrived on the scene. He met with military officers, then departed the next day to report to FDR. His harsh assessment of the preparedness at Pearl, and his descriptions of "the shambles of the Battle Line of the world's mightiest fleet," led to the replacement of both Admiral Kimmel and General Short.

Knox told the president that "neither the Army nor the Navy Commandant in Oahu regarded an air attack on the Army air fields or the Navy Stations as at all likely." Knox's remarks to the American public were not as damaging. He emphasized the heroism of many of the soldiers and civilians who died for their country. Several more investigations of what happened at Pearl Harbor that fateful day occurred through the years. Finally, in 1946, a joint congressional committee released a report laying blame for the ill-preparedness of American forces at the feet of many, from officials in Washington to commanders in Hawaii to intelligence gathering personnel. Even FDR was implicated.

▲ **AN AVIATOR'S RATIONS** were found in a downed plane. The expectation was that if a pilot survived a crash, he would need food to keep him alive in the days before he was found.

▶ **A JAPANESE PILOT WASHED** ashore in the days after the attack. 129 Japanese attackers were killed in the onslaught. One was taken prisoner of war.

Yamamoto had a secret weapon for Pearl Harbor: five midget submarines strapped behind the conning towers of normal subs and towed within range. Each was 78 feet long by 6 feet wide and carried two torpedoes and two crewmen. There never seemed to be any hope, though, that they would be able to inflict real damage; this was basically a suicide mission. Nine of the men in these subs died and were commemorated in the silk painting above, with Ford Island in the center. They became national heroes in Japan, owing to reports that a midget sub had sunk the *Arizona*. The 10th submariner, Sakamaki Kazuo, commanded the sub at left. Kazuo was taken into custody by U.S. forces. According to a December 8, 1941, 14th Naval District Intelligence Office report, the Japanese soldier said, "He wished to commit suicide and had not done so at the time of landing on shore because of the possibility which remained of making his escape and rejoining the Japanese Navy."

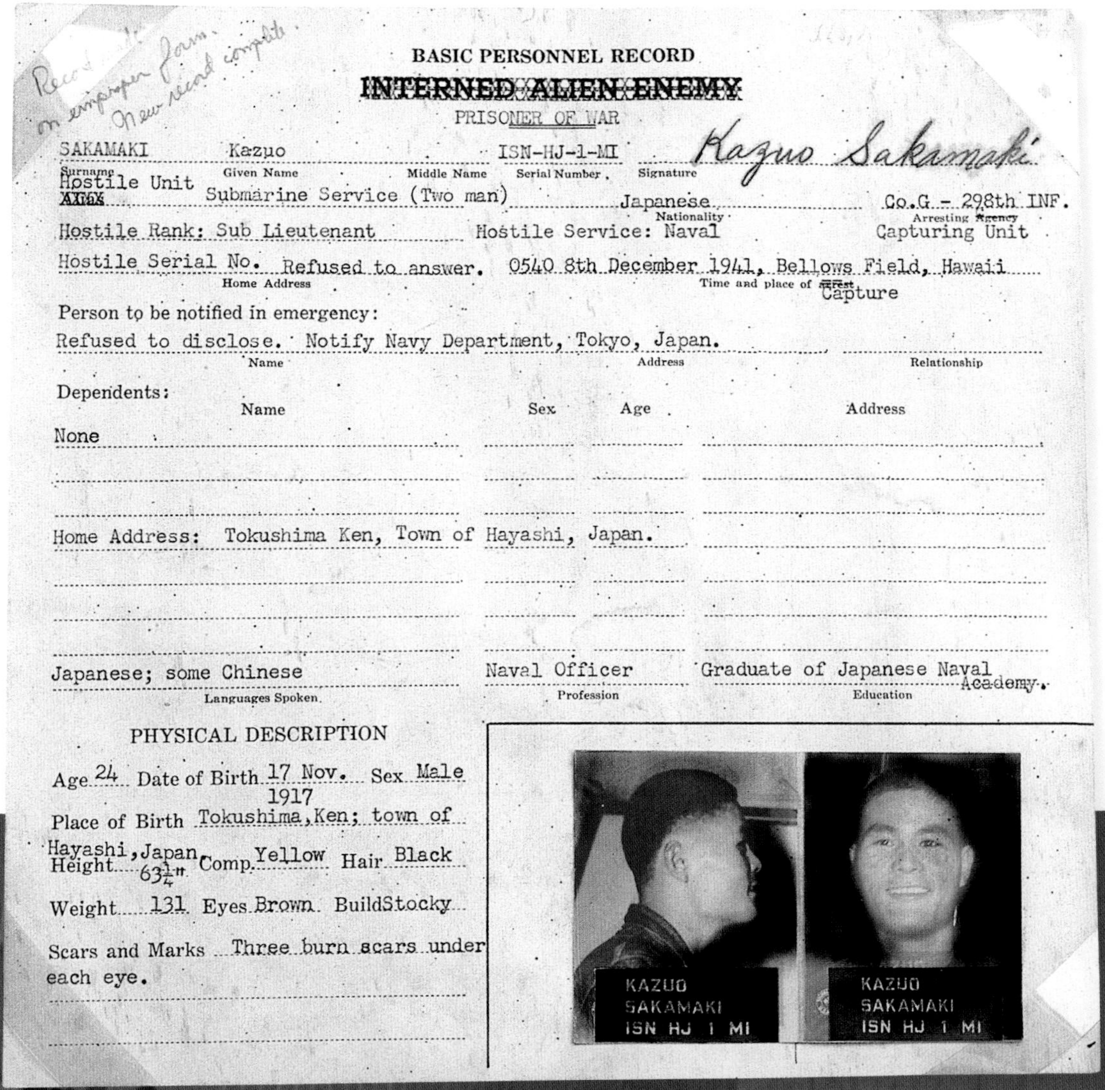

BASIC PERSONNEL RECORD

~~INTERNED ALIEN ENEMY~~

PRISONER OF WAR

SAKAMAKI   Kazuo   ISN-HJ-1-MI   *Kazuo Sakamaki*
Surname   Given Name   Middle Name Serial Number.   Signature

Hostile Unit
~~Alien~~   Submarine Service (Two man)   Japanese   Co.G. - 298th INF.
                                                   Nationality   Arresting Agency

Hostile Rank: Sub Lieutenant   Hostile Service: Naval   Capturing Unit

Hostile Serial No. Refused to answer.   0540 8th December 1941, Bellows Field, Hawaii
                Home Address.   Time and place of ~~First~~ Capture

Person to be notified in emergency:

Refused to disclose. Notify Navy Department, Tokyo, Japan.
                Name   Address   Relationship

Dependents:
                Name   Sex   Age   Address
None

Home Address: Tokushima Ken, Town of Hayashi, Japan.

Japanese; some Chinese   Naval Officer   Graduate of Japanese Naval
        Languages Spoken.   Profession   Education   Academy.

PHYSICAL DESCRIPTION

Age 24. Date of Birth 17 Nov. Sex Male
                      1917
Place of Birth Tokushima,Ken; town of
Hayashi,Japan
Height 63¼" Comp. Yellow Hair Black

Weight 131. Eyes Brown. Build Stocky

Scars and Marks Three burn scars under
each eye.

KAZUO SAKAMAKI ISN HJ 1 MI
KAZUO SAKAMAKI ISN HJ 1 MI

◀ **SAKAMAKI'S SUB** (opposite) suffered from a failed gyroscope and was uncontrollable. Eventually he (and a crewman who died) abandoned ship and washed ashore near Bellows Field, where Sgt. David M. Akui made him America's first prisoner of war in World War II. Note the strikeouts in the form at right, and that one mug shot is a modified version of the photo below.

(Following Pages) **IN HONOLULU** on December 7, these stretcher-bearers rushed a casualty to a makeshift aid station on the grounds of the Lunalilo School, on Pumehana Street. The roof of the school had been set on fire, perhaps by shells from antiaircraft guns. In the foreground, students watch as their school burns.

Fear gripped the people of Hawaii. A *New York Times* story by Lawrence E. Davies, appearing on January 1, 1942, began: "In the last hours of 1941, as the Pacific Coast stayed 'on the alert' against possible holiday surprises by the enemy from sea and air, scores of men wounded in the Japanese raid on Pearl Harbor were brought through the Golden Gate, the second batch of Army and Navy casualties to reach the mainland … Smiling or grim, as they hobbled with crutches or were carried on stretchers from transports, the soldiers and sailors, even those with serious injuries from bomb fragments or bullets, appealed to doctors to 'fix us up quick,' for 'there's work to be done out there next year.' … Some of the wounded recounted their experiences … Typical was the story of J. R. Trammell, aged 20, a farm boy from Oklahoma, who raised his arm on the stretcher as he spoke … 'I was in the crew's galley, and that's where I got mine—shrapnel in both legs. All five boys with me were hit … I'm ready to go back right now.'"

The attack on Pearl Harbor galvanized the American troops and their supporters back home. A wave of patriotism swept the nation as the devastating effects of an attack on American soil took hold of the nation. Suddenly, a nation of people for whom the war was really a distraction became fixated on what could be done "at home" to aid the war effort. From everyday citizens to leaders of industry, sacrifices were made. People learned to live without things from new cars to canned goods as manufacturers retooled auto plants to make airplanes, metals were used for weapons production, and travel was regulated. At one point, shutting down professional baseball was on

▲ THE JAPANESE PLANE THAT CRASHED INTO THIS HOUSE— where a Japanese family resided—was one of the first to be shot down. The Japanese lost 29 aircraft at Pearl Harbor, some shot down by Americans, others crashed or lost at sea.

▲ AN ANTIAIRCRAFT SHELL LANDED NEAR THIS PACKARD IN Honolulu, killing three men from Kaneohe who were headed for their jobs at Pearl Harbor. In all, 68 civilians died in the attack on Pearl Harbor; another 35 were wounded.

the table, lest it seem as if Americans at home were not feeling the woes of war. President Roosevelt himself approved its continuation, citing its effect on positive morale of U.S. citizens. Throughout the nation, women took to the workforce, making the image of Rosie the Riveter a familiar one. Many women took positions in businesses unrelated to wartime as so many men were called to fight. Americans fiercely defended the values of democracy and believed in the value of the war their young men were fighting across the globe.

Despite the surge of patriotism that had Americans rushing to support entry into the war after the attack, the shock of seeing the wounded return home from Pearl Harbor dampened the rising spirits. When several

◄ **AT THE INTERSECTION OF** McCully and King Streets in Honolulu, volunteer firemen fed a hose to a man on this rooftop. Many homes and businesses on the island of Oahu were destroyed by antiaircraft shells fired from American guns that missed their mark.

▼ **WOUNDED TROOPS BEGAN** arriving in San Francisco on Christmas Day, 1941, overflow from the already crowded hospitals on Hawaii. The most gravely wounded had left Oahu in secret on an ocean liner accompanied by Navy cruisers and destroyers.

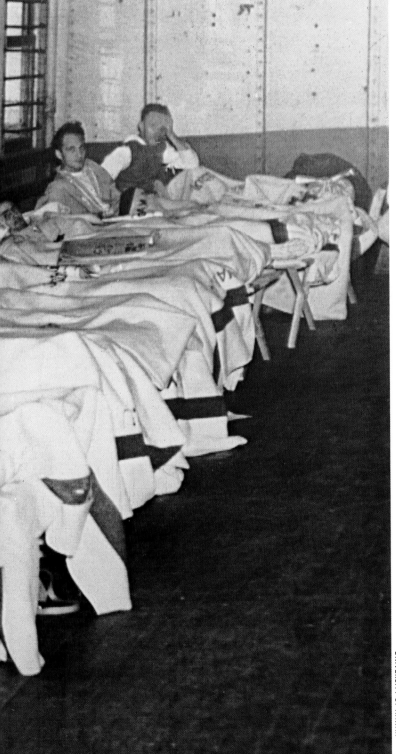

ANNA BUSBY
Lieutenant, Army Nurse Corps

" I went to Hawaii in June 1941. I was a second lieutenant in the Army Nurse Corps, assigned to Tripler Hospital in Honolulu. On December 7, when the Japanese attacked at five minutes to eight, I was actually staying in the hospital as a patient, ambulatory with an infected right cheek.

I remember that the head nurse ran down the hall, which was very unusual, to the back lanai on the second floor—the women's ward. I ran after her. What I saw then was the enormous smoke and fire from Hickam Field and Pearl Harbor. Boom-boom-boom-boom-boom! To our left, something hit the pineapple cannery, and that went up in a huge fire.

The head nurse picked up a phone and called Hickam, then said, 'My God, the Japanese are bombing Pearl Harbor!'

After that I went to the chief nurse. Well, she took one look at me and said, 'Where do you think you're going with that red face? You look like a casualty.' She then ordered me to take care of the women's ward.

There were many patients there already, and then the injured started coming. By 9 a.m., the two lanais were both filled with casualties on litters.

I was truly busy for days. The only thing I can say is, the whole time, I was petrified. When the night nurse came on at 7 p.m. to relieve me on that first day, I was actually too scared to go back to my quarters. I was afraid that I wouldn't be able to speak if the sentry said, 'Halt. Who goes there?' I didn't know if I could answer. So I ended up staying at the hospital.

BUSBY served as the national chair of the White Caps, an organization of Army and Navy nurses who served on Oahu during the attack, from 1969 until her death on May 21, 2010, at the age of 98. She is buried in Montgomery, Alabama. All proceeds from the sale of her autobiography, *Wherever You Need Me*, are donated to benefit the U.S.S. *Arizona* Memorial Fund.

camouflaged U.S. ships approached the Golden Gate Bridge, floating into San Francisco Harbor through the gray mists of a foggy Christmas morning, the eerie sight was a portent of their cargo: the nation's first casualties of World War II. On board the largest luxury liner built in the U.S., the *President Coolidge*, and a smaller Army transport, were 180 men who had been badly wounded at Pearl Harbor, as well as women and children being evacuated from Hawaii. To avoid an attack by Japanese submarines, the ships had slipped out of Oahu with their lights blacked out. Cruisers and destroyers escorted them, and warplanes flew guard above. The convoy had sailed in secret. It had been just 18 days since the Japanese attacked Pearl Harbor, and the

West Coast, which many feared would be the next target, was understandably nervous.

The first San Franciscans to see the convoy were early risers out for a Christmas stroll. Word quickly spread, and soon thousands of people were making their way to the rain-drenched waterfront. Among them were family members of servicemen and -women stationed at Pearl Harbor, who wondered whether their loved ones were on board. Many stateside families still had no idea whether their relatives had survived the attack. When the crowds got within three blocks of the waterfront, they were turned away at barricades by rifle-carrying soldiers and sailors. "Mothers who were wondering whether their sons were aboard stood

(Previous Pages) **IN THE DAYS** after the attack, bodies of civilians and soldiers washed up on the shores around Oahu. Survivors searched the wreckage. This sailor was killed by an air attack at the Naval Air Station on Kanoehe Bay.

▲ **THERE WERE 21 MEN IN** Unit Band 22, the dance orchestra of the U.S.S. *Arizona*. During the attack, all would perish at the band's battle station as they were attempting to pass ammunition under Turrets No. 1 and 2.

in the steady drizzle, watching with hopeful eyes as the passengers emerged," the *San Francisco Chronicle* reported. Ambulances screamed through the crowd and backed up to the ships. When the stretchers began to unload, the horror of the damage inflicted stifled any eager smiles of welcome.

Casualties suffered from a combination of wounds and burns. Almost all the patients suffered from shock in varying degrees. Most of the burn patients had been overboard in the water, and when they came to the hospital or hospital ship they were covered from head to foot with fuel oil. The medics did their best with soap and water, applying local treatment for burns over the oil. Fortunately, the treatment was efficacious.

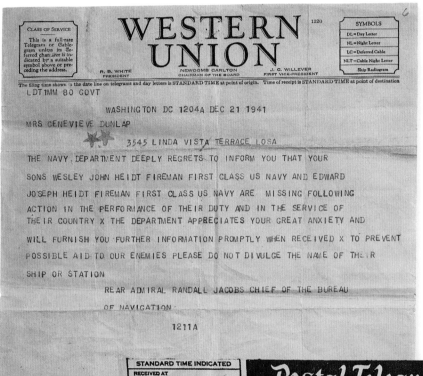

◄ **THE TWO RED STARS ON THE Western Union telegram would also have appeared on the envelope.** They were a wartime signal to the carrier that the telegram contained news that was extremely sensitive to the recipient and accordingly should be delivered with care. These two telegrams refer to the Heidt brothers, pictured above.

(Following Pages) **ONLOOKERS** gathered at the White House for support and direction from their president on what he called "a day that will live in infamy."

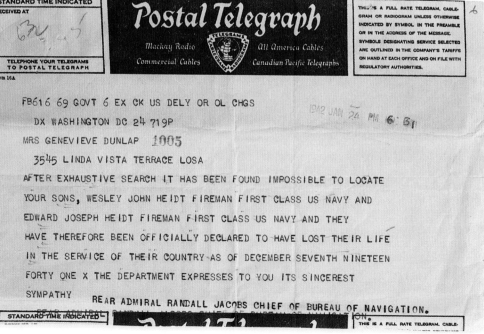

ARMS

Around the globe, reactions to the stunning attack on Pearl Harbor, and attempts to assess what would follow, could not have been more diverse. "We cannot lose the war!" said Adolf Hitler. "Now we have a partner who has not been defeated in three thousand years." The Free French leader Charles de Gaulle, in exile in England, also foresaw an ultimate result, but quite a different one. "The war is over," he said. "Of course there are years of fighting ahead, but the Germans are beaten." For his part, Adm. Yamamoto Isoroku, the architect of the Japanese attack, offered no firm predictions but observed ominously, "I fear all we have done is to awaken a sleeping giant and fill him with a terrible resolve."

The headline in LIFE was "America Goes to War," and the copy read, "In the nation's capital and in cities on both continental coasts the lights of peace flicked off. Troops in steel helmets bared bayonets before the gates of military establishments and areas of arms production. Enemy aliens—Japanese, Italians, Germans—were banged into prisons and detention camps. Interceptor planes stood ready and patrol planes roared ceaselessly along the shores of America's two oceans. Congress prepared to muster a gigantic pool of manpower—10,000,000 men between 19 and 45 for military service; 30,000,000 men up to 65 for

► THE HOUSE OF Representatives crackled with energy on December 8, when Franklin Delano Roosevelt delivered some of the most famous and stirring words in American history. The speech lasted only six minutes but would galvanize a nation. Within an hour, the U.S. was officially at war. Right: Roosevelt's revision of a first draft.

(Previous Pages) AMERICANS answered the bell in droves after the attack. At this New York City recruiting station, 18- and 19-year-olds were sworn in to the Army. Men who volunteered could pick their own branch of service.

DRAFT No. 1   December 7, 1941.

PROPOSED MESSAGE TO THE CONGRESS

Yesterday, December 7, 1941, a date which will live in *infamy*

the United States of America was *suddenly* and deliberately attacked

by naval and air forces of the Empire of Japan.

The United States was at the moment at peace with that nation and was
still in conversations with its Government and its Emperor looking

toward the maintenance of peace in the Pacific. Indeed, one hour after,

Japanese air squadrons had commenced bombing in *Oahu*

the Japanese Ambassador to the United States and his colleague delivered

to the Secretary of State a formal reply to a *recent American* message, from the

While This reply *stated* that diplomatic negotiations

it contained no threat *or* hint of

armed attack.

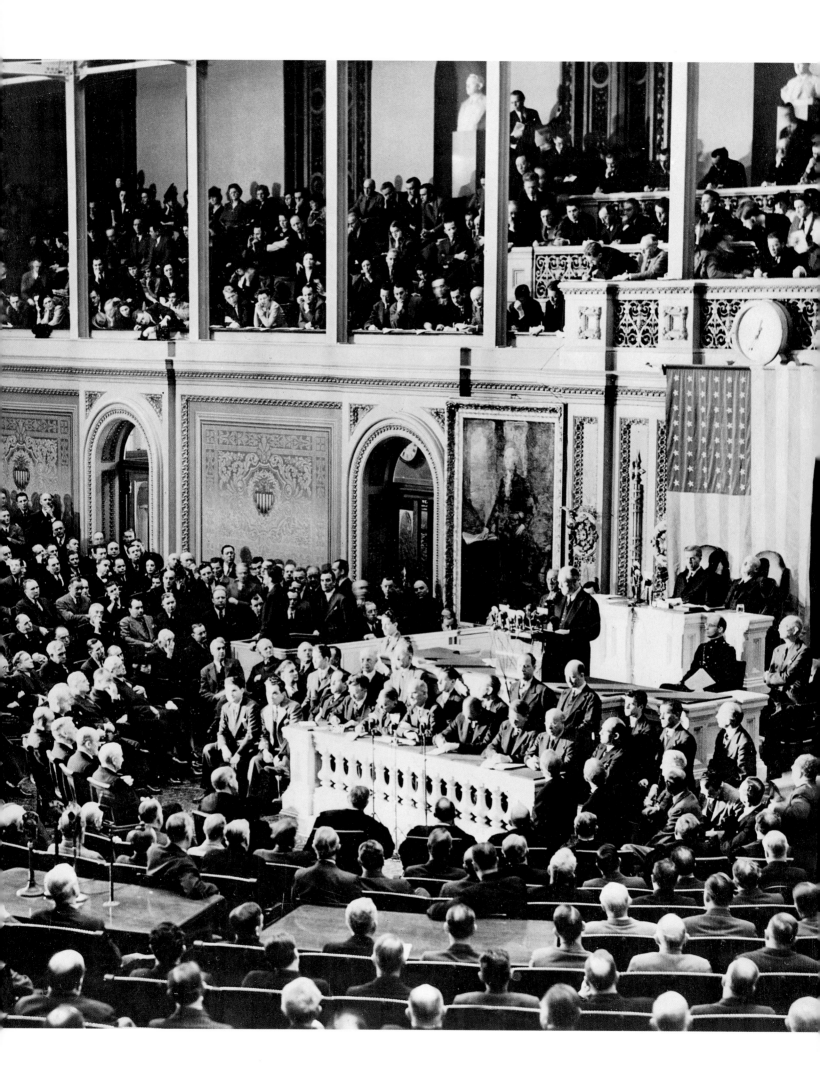

defense activities of all kinds. The ban on overseas duty for selectees was lifted. Air-raid alarms sounded in Seattle, San Francisco, Los Angeles, New York.... At long last two-ocean war had come to America."

Formal declarations were hardly necessary, but in the week following the attack on Pearl Harbor they came fast—and furiously. For the record: On December 8, Japan and the U.S. exchanged pledges to fight to the death. Three days later,

Germany and Italy declared war on the U.S., which returned the favor by nightfall. "Last week war became worldwide," read the *Life* story. "Fighting in Europe, in Africa, in the Far East was merged into the same violent pattern. By week's end there were 33 nations involved, 25 on the side of the Allies, eight with the Axis." While statistically this was true, at the center of the conflict were Britain, the U.S.S.R. and the U.S. vs. Germany, Italy and Japan.

In the near term, Japanese successes in the Pacific augured ill for an Allied offensive in the East. Japan bombed the Philippines, Wake Island and Guam on December 8, while launching invasions of Thailand, Malaya and Hong Kong the same day. It invaded the Gilbert Islands on the 9th and Burma on the 11th. It invaded Borneo on the 16th and initiated a concerted offensive against the Philippines, defended by Gen. Douglas MacArthur's troops, on the 22nd. Japan captured Wake on the 23rd, and on Christmas, Hong Kong surrendered. Japan rang out 1941 with a New Year's Eve occupation of Manila, capital of the Philippines.

The United States was trying to mobilize, but the effort was proving difficult. America's giant industrial machine quickly went on a 24/7 schedule with a goal of a billion dollars in arms a week, but troops had to be trained and strategies formed. On December 10, U.S. aircraft sank a Japanese sub north of Oahu, and five days later a U.S. sub sank the Japanese merchant ship *Atsutasan Maru*. But such individual hits paled in comparison with Japan's dynamic expansion. On January 11, Japan invaded the Dutch East Indies. On the 20th, it pushed its offensive through Burma. On February 15, the crucial port of Singapore surrendered. In March, Japan entered the Burmese capital of Rangoon, accepted the surrender of Java and landed on the Solomon Islands. Meanwhile, MacArthur arrived in Australia from the Philippines, having promised to return—a pledge that appeared, at the time, optimistic.

If the U.S. war effort, particularly in the Pacific, was off to a wheel-spinning start, it wasn't for lack of spirit. "Remember Pearl Harbor!" became the overnight war cry of the American populace, and the press stopped speaking of "defense" in favor of "victory." The America First movement shuttered. Pervasive isolationism had changed to determination to defeat Hitler and defeat the threat of Nazism.

◀ **ANY NOTION OF AMERICAN isolationism** was obliterated by the news from Pearl Harbor. Even longtime critics of FDR knew that the man on the street was ready to take on the enemy. The headline of New York's *Daily Mirror* captured the tenor of the day.

▶ **MEANWHILE, IN JAPAN,** news of the great victory at Pearl Harbor was greeted with enthusiasm, and readers savored the report of Japan's declaration of war.

DMITRI KESSEL/LIFE/THE PICTURE COLLECTION

MAINICHI NEWSPAPERS/AFLO

The rallying cry rang across the country. In New York City, a young man grew impatient waiting in the long line to enlist in the Army. He switched to the Navy line to hurry things along. A Bostonian named Mahoney pinned a note to the wall of the New Haven Railroad engine house where, until he did the pinning, he had been employed. "To my buddies at the roundhouse," Mahoney's note read. "The liberty we enjoy will never be destroyed while boys like you and I can prevent it. That is why I left my job here and enlisted in the United States Marines."

Napoleon once observed, "To be defeated is pardonable; to be surprised—never!" The sentiment was strong among America's military brass in the days following the bombing. Adm. Kimmel clearly knew his fate even as the attack was in progress. He was standing by a window at Naval Command when a spent bullet shattered the glass, nicked him and fell to the floor. Kimmel picked up the slug and said, "It would have been merciful had it killed me."

He was relieved of his duties on December 17 and replaced as head of the Pacific Fleet by Rear Adm. Chester W. Nimitz. "I'm the new commander in chief," Nimitz, in evident distress, told his wife.

"You've wanted this all your life."

"But sweetheart," said Nimitz, "all the ships are at the bottom."

That wasn't quite so, and this made all the difference. As devoted as Yamamoto had been to the idea of a sneak attack, he was consistently reluctant to embrace any suggestion of a follow-up strike on Pearl. The Japanese had a golden opportunity to improve on their formal plans when Commander Fuchida, flush with success, implored Adm. Nagumo to okay a second mass aerial attack. Nagumo said no. His carriers turned for Japan. The Japanese had made a crucial mistake. Over the next four years, the forces of the United States would come roaring back to defeat Japan.

▲ **WOMEN WORKED ALONGSIDE MEN IN FEBRUARY 1942 ON THIS** assembly line in Cincinnati that made armor-piercing shells. As men shipped out, women stepped in, big-time: In 1941, they made up just 1 percent of all aviation employees; by 1943, they accounted for 65 percent. "Rosie the Riveter" had become vital.

THE DOOLITTLE RAID

WHILE THE MILITARY SCRAMBLED TO FINE-tune itself for war, FDR recognized the need for an immediate poultice to ease the psychic wound Pearl Harbor had inflicted on the American people. He and his military advisors decided to mount an offensive against Tokyo, to strike at the heart of the enemy. An elaborate offensive was planned, involving a tactic that would make military history: he launching of heavy, long-range bombers directly off the decks of carrier ships. This required an enhanced level of piloting skills, as new techniques were required for "short field takeoffs" and maneuvering in oceanic weather conditions. Also, although the planes could take off from the deck, they couldn't re-land there, so the raiders had to find safe places for landing after they had dropped their bombs. Onto this dramatic stage of combat strode a much-needed star, a charismatic and brilliant soldier whose heroics gave America a badly needed surge of pride and patriotism: **Lt. Col. James "Jimmy" Doolittle**. The son of an Alaskan gold prospector, a former boxer and flying daredevil, Doolittle held a doctorate in aeronautic engineering from MIT. On April 18, 1942, under his command, 16 U.S. Army bombers were launched from the deck of the aircraft carrier U.S.S. *Hornet* toward Tokyo, where they targeted military and industrial compounds. Each plane carried four 500-pound bombs. Though in the full scheme of the war the strike was slight, the morale boost for the U.S. was huge. It created a war hero, showed how vulnerable the Japanese islands were to attack, and set in motion a chain of events that, in the end, proved disastrous for the Japanese war effort.

LT. COL. DOOLITTLE (fifth from left) with members of his flight crew and Chinese officials in China after the Doolittle Raid. To the right is Chao Foo Ki, secretary of the Western Chekiang Province Branch Government.

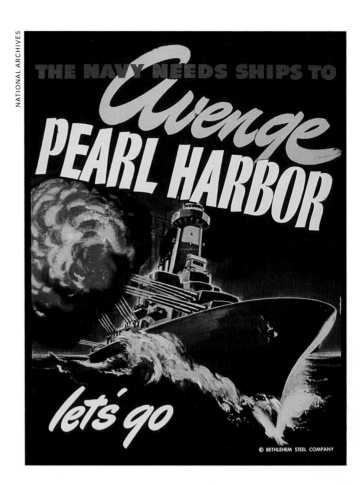

They hadn't finished off Pearl Harbor.

Vulnerable at Pearl Harbor were several damaged but not destroyed battleships, intact repair facilities and a massive cluster of oil tanks filled with fuel. Returning to Pearl from a mission to Wake Island was the U.S.S. *Enterprise*, which would have presented a prime target. That all of these assets were spared proved vital when, in early May 1942, the Japanese suffered setbacks during the Battle of the Coral Sea. Precisely a month later, the U.S. Pacific Fleet scored perhaps the greatest naval victory ever at the Battle of Midway, where it halted Japan's eastward push and let the Axis know that the fight was now well and truly engaged.

The Battle of Midway was the first major defeat suffered by the Japanese navy in 350 years. The results had a massive effect on the psychological profile of the war. What would end with atomic bombings began, of course, at Pearl Harbor. But it began again at Midway.

◄ ON MARCH 1, 1942, THE cruiser *Houston* was sunk by the Japanese during the Battle of Sunda Strait. All 1,068 aboard were killed or taken prisoner. Not long after, Navy recruits who had enlisted to avenge the ship's loss, filled this plaza in Houston, Texas, for their swearing-in.

▲ IN POSTERS, SPEECHES, movies and song, "Pearl Harbor" became synonymous with "sneak attack." Propaganda was used to stoke patriotism among the nation's citizens. Most posters were produced by the Office of War Information, formed in June 1942.

Much of the Navy's success was owed to code breaking. Unlike the German codes like Enigma, which were mechanical ciphers, the Japanese used book ciphers, wherein common words and phrases were replaced with a group of numbers and codes. Acting on intelligence reports, Adm. Chester W. Nimitz gathered ships that had survived Pearl Harbor and the Coral Sea, and ambushed the Japanese fleet at the western tip of the Hawaiian chain in June 1942.

During the Battle of Midway, the U.S.S. *Yorktown* was sunk and more than 300 American seamen perished. However, the Japanese navy was rocked by the loss of four carriers, all of which had participated at Pearl.

U.S. NAVY

NATIONAL ARCHIVES

◀ **THE *HIRYU* ATTEMPTING** to avoid high-level bombing. (Top) **Survivors of the *Hiryu*** were picked up in a lifeboat two weeks later by the *Ballard*.

▲ **DAUNTLESS DIVE-BOMBERS** from the *Hornet* approached the burning cruiser *Mikuma*. U.S. forces were determined to defeat the Japanese.

THE CALL TO ARMS 143

Not all battleships made it to Midway. During Pearl Harbor, the U.S.S. *West Virginia* was struck by two bombs and at least seven torpedoes. Leaking fuel for 30 hours, it eventually caught fire. Tragically, sailors were trapped inside the great ship as it sank, some surviving for as many as 16 days until they perished, rescue crews unable to reach them. The ship was finally hauled to dry dock on June 9, when the bodies of 66 crew members were found.

The *West Virginia* remained out of commission until the Battle of Surigao Strait in the Philippines in October 1944, when it played a vital role in what would be the last time battleships would square off in any war, anywhere. The "Wee Vee" also participated in operations at Iwo Jima and Okinawa, and was in Toyko Bay for the final surrender. In 1947, the great warship was decommissioned. In 1959, she was broken up and sold for scrap metal, a sorrowful ending for the noble ship.

BOB LANDRY/LIFE/THE PICTURE COLLECTION

U.S. NAVY (2)

◄ **THE *WEST VIRGINIA* IN DRY** dock at the Navy Yard. The damage sustained at Pearl Harbor kept her out of most of the war, but her presence at key battles earned her five battle stars.

▲ **THE U.S.S. *ARIZONA* COULD** not be revived (top), but with work by divers like these, most of the ship's guns were recovered and many were put back into service.

The U.S.S. *Oklahoma* was capsized beyond repair and had to be moved to clear an important berth at the port, which would continue to play a major staging role in the war. The Japanese decision to forgo a final attack was a critical error. Oil tanks containing 4.5 million barrels of precious fuel could have provided the Japanese with a decisive victory had they been targeted, as without them the Pacific Fleet would have been forced back to the West Coast, seriously impeding offensive operations.

The U.S.S. *Nevada* was the only battleship to get under way during the attack at Pearl. She returned to combat in May 1943 and took part in many major operations. Through the months and years that have followed Pearl Harbor and Midway, certain names have carried import that will stir souls as long as history endures: Tarawa... Guadalcanal... The Gilbert, Marshall and Mariana Islands... New Guinea... Saipan... Burma... Leyte Gulf... Iwo Jima... Okinawa... and at last, on September 2, 1945, the U.S.S. *Missouri*, scene of the formal Japanese surrender in Tokyo Bay.

THESE PICTURES SHOW TWO stages in the herculean effort to right and refloat the capsized *Oklahoma*. The "first pull" of the ship took place on March 8.

(Following Pages) **ON APRIL 19, 1942, the *Nevada* prepared** to steam to Puget Sound for further repairs and modernization.

ITHIN

T
he fallout from the attack was immediate and multifaceted. As Charles Hirshberg writes, one manifestation—the internment of innocent Japanese-Americans—was more than unfortunate. It was ugly.

Within 12 hours of the attack across the Pacific in Hawaii, it seemed as though a bomb had fallen on Yoshiko Uchida's northern California home. "A strange man sat in our living room," Uchida would later recall, "and my father was gone."

It would have been hard to imagine a family more innocuous than the Uchidas. Yoshiko's mother, Iku, kept house, cooked scrumptious sukiyaki and, as a hobby, collected dolls. Yoshiko's father, Dwight, an assistant manager at an import-export firm, grew white chrysanthemums and prizewinning gladiolas in the front yard. Yoshiko was a senior at the University of California at Berkeley, an American citizen who had grown up drinking from a Little Orphan Annie mug and romping around Alameda County with her collie, Laddie.

Nonetheless, on December 7, 1941, the Uchidas were considered enemies of the United States, and so Dwight was led away while the "strange man"—an FBI agent—continued to guard Iku and Yoshiko. Within months, the rest of the family would be ushered to an assembly center at the Tanforan

(Previous Page) **IN THE Manzanar camp, three young detainees were posed at a barbed wire fence by fellow inmate Toyo Miyatake, a Los Angeles photographer who had fashioned a wooden camera out of a lens and film holder that he had snuck past the guards.**

▲ **NEARLY HALF THE JAPANESE** interned during the war were children. Life for children in the camps was especially difficult and many were separated from their families. Years later, the health problems from the trauma experienced would plague an inordinate number.

▲ IN APRIL 1942, A TRAIN PACKED WITH JAPANESE-Americans from San Pedro, California, arrived at the Santa Anita center, the system's largest, which at one point housed 18,719 people on the grounds of an erstwhile racetrack.

Race Track in San Bruno, California, for assignment to one of 10 camps—prisons—designed to house Japanese-Americans during the war. Years later Yoshiko would still remember their quarters at Tanforan: a horse stall that stank of manure. It had been hastily whitewashed; crumpled corpses of spiders were stuck to the walls.

It happened with stunning speed for the Uchidas and very fast for most Japanese Americans. With the attack on Pearl Harbor, many male noncitizens who had been born in Japan, like Dwight Uchida, were immediately rounded up, and calls for the imprisonment of everyone with Japanese blood—U.S. citizen or not—were instantly in the air. Secretary of the Navy Frank Knox, desperately trying to shift the blame for the disaster at Pearl Harbor, led the call for lockup, insisting that an "effective fifth column" of Japanese-Americans had somehow aided the Japanese attack. The fever spread. "Herd 'em up, pack 'em off and give 'em the inside room in the badlands," wrote Henry McLemore in his Hearst-chain column. "Let 'em be pinched, hurt, hungry and dead up against it.... And that goes for all of them."

While some level-headed government officials pleaded for calm, others pressed for action, both to stem espionage activities that Japanese-Americans might be engaged in and to protect them from the worst impulses of their neighbors.

California congressman Leland Ford, whose state was home to the great majority of the nation's 127,000 Japanese-Americans, telephoned the U.S. Attorney General's office and, as Ford later recalled, "I told them to stop f---ing around. I gave them twenty four hours' notice that unless they would issue a mass evacuation notice I would...give the bastards everything [I] could with both barrels."

On February 19, 1942, Roosevelt signed Executive Order 9066, a law enabling the eventual "relocation" to other states or to internment camps of 120,000 West Coast Japanese-Americans, citizens and resident aliens alike. The presumption was that those nearest the Pacific would be of most use to the Japanese military and should therefore be moved inland.

The detainees were instructed to bring only what they could carry to one of 16 assembly centers—compounds thrown together at fairgrounds, racetracks, even a stockyard in Portland, Oregon. The prisoners traveled in a daze, surrounded by armed military guards. William Marutani, then a student at the University of Washington, was so stunned that he blanked out completely. "I literally don't remember the trip," he said years later. "I formed a mental block and just shut down." "It had never occurred to us that we might be picked up," says George Aratani, who was, at the time, a 24-year-old produce supplier in the Santa Maria Valley in

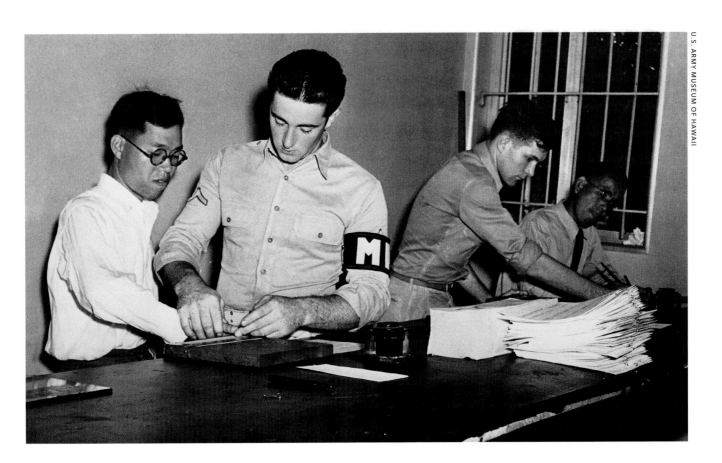

U.S. ARMY MUSEUM OF HAWAII

▲ DETAINEES WERE FINGERPRINTED IN HONOLULU IN FEBRUARY 1942. They would eventually be interned at one of 17 sites in Hawaii between 1942 and 1945.

RONALD OBA
High School Student

"Before the war, the Japanese on Hawaii were mostly immigrants working for the sugar plantations. They had come to make some money and return to Japan. We had many little towns—a Japanese village, a Philippine camp, a Chinese camp, a Portuguese camp, a Spanish camp. We had all kinds of people and got along really well, except for the Caucasians. They always had their own section with their tennis courts and swimming pools.

My parents had arrived around 1914. They ran a barber shop, and I and my six brothers and sisters grew up in Oahu about a quarter of a mile from the north shore of Pearl Harbor. We used to swim and fish in Pearl Harbor. At that time there were no restrictions about rowing your boat next to a submarine or a destroyer.

On Sundays, we always had hot cakes. It was a treat. All of a sudden I heard this 'Bang-bang-bang.' It went from one end of the horizon to the other. 'Boom, boom!' I said to my family. 'Oh, they are having maneuvers again.' Then there was a 'rhruunmp' and a great explosion shook our flimsy home.

Still in my pajamas, I jumped up and ran down to the shore. I was there in five minutes. The water was lapping my feet as I was watching. I said, 'My God, the battleship *Arizona* is on fire.' Another battleship started to burn. Early in the morning there is no wind, and the black clouds and the smoke were just going straight up like a mushroom.

I said, 'What is happening?' I looked up and saw swarms of Zeros in the air. I couldn't even hear the drone of the planes because there were so many explosions. I saw a dive-bomber coming from the Waikiki area into Battleship Row. I actually saw it drop a torpedo. Instead of pulling up, the bomber turned and hugged the surface of the water and came directly at me. I saw the pilot's face—he had a canvas type of a helmet and large goggles. He was looking down at me.

As I was standing on shore, a truckload of Marines came up. They yelled at me to go home. I ran back home and they secured the beaches.

That night every house had to be blacked out. If a single ray of light came out, then the house was shot at. Everybody was so scared. Our parents were so afraid, they burned everything that had to do with Japan. Samurai swords were buried under the house. We had shortwave radios, and were told to break them up. We made a bonfire in the yard and were burning and burying things.

The next day ships were coming back and forth, unloading dead bodies. There was a concrete pier. The sailors' bodies were piled high like cords.

We were immediately charged as enemy aliens. Any Japanese, whether American or not, was declared an enemy.

Eventually I went to work for the Navy, building ammunition magazines. I fought with the Japanese-American 442nd Regimental Combat Team in Italy and France. Every parent told us not to come back home—to uphold the samurai-bushido upbringing by dying gloriously."

AFTER the war Oba earned a master's in hospital administration and oversaw Hilo Hospital on the Big Island until retiring in 1987. He is now 93. In 2010 the Senate unanimously passed a bill to award the Congressional Gold Medal to Oba and 6,000 other Japanese-Americans who fought for the U.S. in World War II.

California. "We were Americans." Aratani decided to try to retain ownership of his company during his detention, but many other businessmen sold out hastily, usually for a pittance. Other possessions, too, were sold or forfeited. A white woman stopped by the Uchidas' house and asked if she might dig up Dwight's gladiolas. "Since you're leaving anyway," the woman offered helpfully.

The first camp to open was Manzanar, and with its eventual population of 10,000 it became, for a time, the largest city between L.A. and Reno. The Uchidas were sent from Tanforan to the Topaz camp in Utah. In February, 12 members of the Miyahara family were processed at Tanforan for transport to the Topaz camp as well. Flo Miyahara, 18 at the time, still remembers the experience vividly: her large family jammed into two rooms of a tar-paper shack at the racetrack. Flo was told to fill a sack with straw; this would

be her new bed. She did so, then went outside and walked to the fence that surrounded Tanforan. "I couldn't believe where I was," she says now. "I just stood there staring at the road, watching the cars drive by. All my life, I had been free to go where I wanted; now I wasn't, and I just couldn't understand why. I couldn't stop watching the cars. After many hours, my family had to actually pry my fingers from the fence."

George Aratani was sent out of state. "The windows on the train were closed and the shades were drawn," he remembers. "We were told not to look out, but we were curious. Whenever someone tried to peek through, a soldier would shout, 'Hey, you! Keep away from that window!'" When the train finally halted, Aratani was shocked to find himself in the Arizona desert. Two camps, which together would eventually house 15,000, had been built on the Gila

▲ **AMID DRY, DUSTY CONDITIONS, JAPANESE-AMERICANS**
arrived at Manzanar, where they were assigned to rustic barracks.

River Indian Reservation. The camps were extremely overcrowded, with as many as 25 people living in a space designed for four.

Bob Sakata was 16 when he arrived at the similarly desolate and crowded Topaz camp. He was trying to believe that he was being relocated in part for his own safety. But one look at the camp guards and he knew it was a lie: "I thought, if they're here to protect us, their guns should be pointing out, away from us. But they weren't."

By October 1942, 100,000 detainees were living in 10 camps scattered throughout the West. Most compounds were surrounded by barbed wire, watchtowers and sentries. By design, the locations of the camps were remote; most were in the desert, where harsh winds whipped dust through cracks in the walls of the crude barracks. Preserving food in this environment was difficult, and illness spread. Almost no preparation had been made by authorities to provide for the health of the prisoners or to educate the thousands of children now under guard.

The inmates, therefore, shouldered new responsibilities. Those with training in first aid became nurses. The college-educated, like Yoshiko Uchida, became school teachers. At first, classes were held without the benefit of desks or chairs. Yoshiko remembered snakes slithering in from the desert and having to send children home in tempests of dust: a very different kind of snow day.

In many camps, students dutifully began each day with the Pledge of Allegiance, followed by a chorus of "My Country, 'Tis of Thee." "There was a terrible combination of concern and depression, but my father was always telling us: Try to prove you're worthy of being in this country," says Sakata.

As he implies, the psychological wounds inflicted on the prisoners ran deeper than any physical effects of their deprivation. Though they had done no wrong, many began to blame themselves. "America was our mother, the only mother we had," explains William Marutani, who was imprisoned at Tule Lake, California, until he succeeded in joining the Army in 1944. "You start to think, 'If my mother's doing this to me, she must have a damn good reason.'"

"Hardest hit were the women," says Cherry Tsutsumida, who spent three years of her childhood in a camp on the Gila River. "I used to hear them crying at night. Mothers had no idea what was going on: What had they done wrong? I was nine, and these women would ask me to teach them to read English, so they could understand things better. They were too embarrassed to ask the older kids, so we'd sit and read my little book.

"It was like being raped, and then being treated like everything that happened was your fault. You began to feel ashamed."

One day, Flo Miyahara snapped at her mother: "You shouldn't have had children! Then we wouldn't be here!" Not long after, Flo and some friends made a pathetic attempt to escape. They got as far as a local train station before they were caught by soldiers. "One was named Lieutenant Nails. He kicked one of our guys and said, 'If you move, I'll blow a hole in you as big as a barn.'" Some prisoners actually were shot, including Shoichi James Okamoto of Garden Grove, California, who was killed during an altercation with a

AP

◀ IN MARCH 1942, NEW arrivals at Manzanar made beds of straw. Eventually the camp would hold more than 10,000 people, organized into 36 blocks with 12 barracks in each block.

HANSEL MIETH/LIFE/THE PICTURE COLLECTION

sentry at the Tule Lake camp; James Hatsuki Wakasa, who reportedly tried to escape from the Manzanar camp; and at least half a dozen others. An Army officer at Manzanar reported to an official that sentries "were finding guard service very monotonous, and that nothing would suit them better than to have a little excitement, such as shooting a Jap."

The most vicious attitudes began to change as the war went on and the public came to realize that the detainees were not a threat to the nation. Not least, thousands of Japanese-Americans were buying credibility by performing nobly in the armed services. Twenty-five thousand Japanese-Americans volunteered for duty in World War II; 4,000 of them came from the camps. In the fall of 1943, the 100th Battalion, a Hawaiian National Guard unit composed of ethnic Japanese, served so heroically in the Italian campaign that it became known as the Purple Heart Battalion. The 442nd Regimental Combat Team—made up in great

measure of men recruited from the camps—became one of the most decorated units in the U.S. military, garnering a Congressional Medal of Honor, 47 Distinguished Service Crosses, 350 Silver Stars, 810 Bronze Stars and more than 3,600 Purple Hearts. President Truman would later congratulate these soldiers for fighting against "not only the enemy, but prejudice."

Beginning in 1943, some prisoners were quietly discharged from the camps. In June 1944, Interior Secretary Harold Ickes advised President Roosevelt that "the continued retention of these innocent people ... would be a blot upon the history of this country." With an upcoming election, Roosevelt demurred "for the sake of internal quiet." However, on December 17, 1944, with FDR's reelection a fait accompli, a public proclamation was issued declaring that the government had "carefully examined" more than 115,000 Japanese-Americans—including 20,000 under age 14—and concluded that they should be "allowed to enjoy

CARL MYDANS/LIFE/THE PICTURE COLLECTION

▲ **THE CAMPS DIFFERED IN SIZE BUT NOT IN DESIGN: BLOCKS** consisting of 12 barracks, perhaps half a dozen rooms per barrack, about 400 square feet each and housing at least one family per room. The Hosokawas dressed up their quarters at the Heart Mountain Relocation Center in northwestern Wyoming as best they could.

▶ **THIS JAPANESE AMERICAN INTERNED AT TULE LAKE PASSED THE** time playing his guitar. This part of the camp segregated those who had resisted internment. It also housed German and Italian prisoners of war. Today, a restoration project is in the works to commemorate those who suffered there.

the same privileges accorded other law-abiding American citizens or residents." One of the most ignoble chapters in America's wartime history was ended.

Despite their accomplishments, all former detainees would carry scars as they made their way in a society that had treated them harshly. William Marutani, who died in 2014, became a lawyer and judge in Philadelphia, a member of the Commission on Wartime Relocation and Internment of Civilians, and a longtime advocate for civil rights. He was the first Japanese-American to gain a judicial appointment outside the West Coast and Hawaii. Bob Sakata of Denver became a farmer, founding Sakata Farms and, along with his wife, Joanna, being inducted into both the Colorado Agricultural and the Colorado Business Halls of Fame. Dr. Flo Miyahara, who died in 2011, devoted her life to pediatrics in Denver. Cherry Tsutsumida worked for Senator Ted Kennedy's office as a Congressional Fellow. George Aratani, who died in 2013, was an entrepreneur and philanthropist who founded two corporations: Mikasa, the dinnerware and crystal company, and Kenwood, the electronics giant. He and his wife endowed the nation's first academic chair to study the World War II internment of people of Japanese descent and their efforts to gain redress. Yoshiko Uchida became an author. Before her death in 1992, she wrote numerous charming children's books, such as *The Dancing Kettle* and *Two Foolish Cats*. She also wrote *The Invisible Thread*, which is based in part on her experiences at the Utah compound.

In 1983, the Commission on Wartime Relocation and Internment of Civilians, having conducted an investigation, recommended that Congress make reparations to those who spent time in the camps. Five years later, America officially apologized for its actions. In 1990, Congress started to pay $1.25 billion to survivors. On June 29, 2001, the National Japanese-American Memorial to Patriotism opened in Washington, D.C. A bronze statue depicts two 14-foot cranes, wings spread as they free themselves from a tangle of barbed wire. Inscribed on the wall behind is a history of Japanese-Americans in wartime, as well as the names of soldiers who died in World War II—a war during which, it is interesting to note, not a single known act of espionage was committed by a Japanese-American.

George Aratani, when asked if he remained as patriotic as ever, was surprised by the question. "Sure," he replied. "Why not? Just because the United States kicked us around doesn't make us any less American."

◀ **AT THE RELOCATION CENTER IN HEART MOUNTAIN, WYOMING,** some of the 12,000 Japanese-American internees saluted their country's flag in 18-degree weather. The camp foreman, noting cracks in the walls of the ramshackle barracks, said, "Well, I guess those Japs will be stuffing their underwear in there to keep the wind out."

9 PEARL HARBOR

TODAY

"It is my earnest hope and indeed the hope of all mankind that from this solemn occasion a better world shall emerge out of the blood and carnage of the past."

— GEN. DOUGLAS MACARTHUR, SEPTEMBER 2, 1945

The serene bay was once known for the pearl oysters that grew in its waters. Since the late 1800s, when Hawaii's King Kalakaua gave the U.S. permission to develop there, the area has been known as a base of naval operations. Since December 7, 1941, the harbor has been known for one thing above all. Seventy-five years after the attack, Pearl Harbor remains a place of solemn pilgrimage. In 1958 President Eisenhower declared it a National Monument, funded by both the public sector and by private donors. In 1961, fresh from a two-year stint in the Army, Elvis Presley gave a benefit concert at Pearl Harbor's Block Arena, raising more than $50,000—more than 10 percent of the final cost of the Memorial. It now attracts over a million visitors a year, many of whom are Japanese. In fact, Japanese tourism accounts for a healthy percentage of Hawaii's income.

History, like a game of musical chairs, has shifted its players. Japan, Germany, and the United States are now allies, uneasily watching the rumblings of Russia, North Korea, and China. Hostilities endure, but the uniforms change. What has also changed is the very nature of war itself. The atom bomb that ended World War II also ended our fundamental expectation of security. The existence of weapons of mass destruction has mired the world in a moral quandary that may have begun with Nagasaki.

(Previous Page) **ONE THOUSAND ONE HUNDRED AND SEVENTY-seven sailors and Marines were entombed in the U.S.S.** *Arizona* **on December 7, 1941. Their names are inscribed on this marble wall at the** *Arizona* **Memorial. It has come to commemorate all military personnel who died during the attack. There were 333 survivors.**

(Above and left) **THE NATIONAL MEMORIAL CEMETERY OF THE Pacific, aka Punchbowl, on Memorial Day.** Almost half of the Americans who died at Pearl Harbor are buried here. The cemetery sits in a crater formed 75,000 years ago by volcanic activity on the island. Its Hawaiian name, *Puowaina*, means "hill of sacrifice." The remains of soldiers who fought throughout the Pacific theater were buried at Punchbowl beginning in 1949. The cemetery has become a popular tourist destination.

Robert J. Oppenheimer, director of the Manhattan Project at Los Alamos, was so repulsed by what he considered the unnecessary dropping of the second bomb that he hand-delivered a letter of protest to Harry L. Stimson, the secretary of war. Oppenheimer enraged Truman by declaring that he felt he had "blood on his hands" for creating the bomb, and he implored the president to ban nuclear weapons. Truman threw Oppenheimer out of his office and told his undersecretary of state, Dean Acheson, "I don't want to see that son of a bitch in this office ever again."

In the aftermath of the war, the U.S. hoped to maintain a monopoly on nuclear warfare, but secrets and technology spread quickly during the Cold War. The era of espionage came to fruition.

Four years after the bombs were dropped in Japan, the Soviet Union conducted its first nuclear test explosion. The United Kingdom, France, and China followed. In 1968 the Nuclear Nonproliferation Treaty was established to keep the technology contained. In 1996 the Comprehensive Nuclear Test Ban Treaty was enacted. Article VI of the treaty states that each state-party is to "pursue negotiations in good faith on effective measures relating to cessation of the nuclear arms race at an early date and to nuclear disarmament." Today, despite efforts to rein in the potential for

SEPTEMBER 11, 2001

PEARL HARBOR NO LONGER HOLDS THE distinction of being the sole site of a surprise attack on America. On September 11, 2001, on a sunny Tuesday morning, four American planes were hijacked in mid-air by 19 terrorists associated with the Islamic extremist group al-Qaeda. Two of the planes crashed into the twin towers of the World Trade Center in Manhattan. The third hit the Pentagon, just outside Washington, D.C. The fourth was thwarted by the extraordinary courage of a group of passengers, who fought the terrorists and managed to crash the plane into a field in Pennsylvania, where there were no survivors. The final death count of the day's attacks was almost 3,000. Immediately after the stunned realization that America had been attacked, the outrage of Pearl Harbor was resurrected. And just as the populace rallied after the first day of Infamy, so Americans came together on 9/11, with an outpouring of courage, selflessness, and unification.

A FIREFIGHTER SEARCHES the wreckage at the World Trade Center. The search and recovery effort went on for months, but the last person pulled out alive was found around 12:30 p.m. the day after the attack.

STEVE MCCURRY/MAGNUM

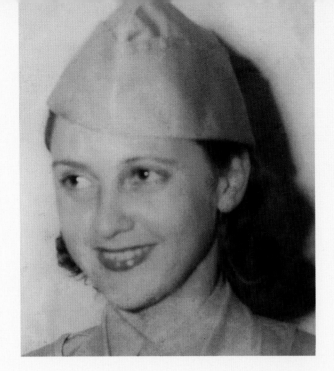

ELIZABETH MCINTOSH

Reporter, *Honolulu Star-Bulletin*

"There was oil in the water, and the smell. The buildings all flattened and rubble. The ships so silent."

"I got up early and put on the radio. It was the Mormon Tabernacle Choir. All of a sudden this man's voice crackled over and said, 'The islands are under attack. This is the real McCoy.' Then the radio went off and I said, 'Oh, more war games.' The military was always doing games. They would pretend to be attacking the island. I then got a phone call from my photographer, 'Hump' Campbell. He asked if I would like to come on in: 'There's something happening. I'm not sure what.'

On the way in, no one was tense or anything. We were going along wonderful sunny streets. People were walking their dogs or going to church. Some people were playing tennis or shopping. It was an every-Sunday type of leisurely morning.

That all changed when we arrived in Honolulu. We heard sirens. We could feel the tenseness. There was nobody in the streets. First thing we found was an open market filled with Christmas stuff. Antiaircraft shells had knocked it flat. There were tinsel, ribbons, cards and toys around. In the middle of it was this little kid. He was having a wonderful time with all these toys.

It was madness at the *Star-Bulletin*. I asked to be assigned to Pearl. They said, 'No, women are not allowed to go out there.' I was assigned to go to Queens Hospital. At that point the nurses and doctors were putting tape on the windows because they were afraid there might be more bombing. The first people who came in were the Hickam Field firemen. I can just see them, being carried in on stretchers, coming down this long corridor. They were blackened and bleeding. A lot of the men were unconscious. Some of them were groaning.

This was around 10 o'clock. I stayed there all day getting stories, then walked back to the office. There was just complete desolation: The whole city was closed down except for the police and the sirens.

I got the stuff out for Scripps-Howard papers, but then found out that the censorship had set in and you could not send anything by wire out of Honolulu.

I got out to Pearl a couple of days later. All along the streets there were dead mynah birds and doves and sparrows. The concussion from the bombs had killed them. At Pearl it was horrible—that whole awful scene. There was oil in the water, and the smell. The buildings all flattened and rubble. The ships so silent. I remember, at the *Arizona*, the air bubbles bubbling up from below. It could have been people. There were 1,000 men or something like that down below."

THOUGH McIntosh was assigned to cover the day's events "from a woman's point of view," her piece was never published, because the editor was nervous about her graphic descriptions of blood-soaked children and other victims. However, the *Washington Post* published the article in full in 2012, to commemorate the 71st anniversary of Pearl Harbor. In it, she writes of all the phone calls she received that day from women stuck at home, anxious to know what they could do to help. "It was then that I realized," she wrote, "how important women can be in a war torn world."

In 1941, McIntosh was writing for both the *Star-Bulletin* and the Scripps-Howard News Service. During the war she worked for the OSS in India and China; afterward she was employed variously by Voice of America, the United Nations and the CIA. She was married three times; the first marriage ended in divorce, and she was widowed twice. She had no children. She died at the age of 100 on June 8, 2015, in Virginia.

RAYMOND EMORY
Seaman, U.S.S. *Honolulu*

"I can remember it like it was just yesterday. I was reading a newspaper at my bunk, one deck below topside. General quarters sounded. Naturally everybody headed for their battle stations. I got to the .50-caliber machine guns. I was the first one there and started pulling the covers off. I had one all of the way off and another about halfway off when the first plane went by our stern. When the second plane went by, I noticed the big red ball. That was when I realized what was going on.

The ammunition box was locked at the machine gun. I didn't know who had the keys and didn't care anyway. I just had to get the damn thing opened. I used a dog wrench, a piece of pipe, to break the box open. After we got the box open and the machine guns manned, we fired at anything that came close.

When you are firing a machine gun you kind of get tunnel vision. You are concentrating on what you are firing at, and you are not seeing anything to the left or right. I only saw this one plane go down: The prop came off of the nose and kept on going, but the torpedo plane just stopped in the middle of the air, lit like a Christmas tree, and down it went. That was the only airplane I saw go down, and everybody and his brother were firing at it.

The only noise that I remember was a three-inch gun right below us. When that thing went, I never heard anything else. When a big bang goes off near your ears, you don't hear for quite a while. I never heard the *Arizona* blowing up, or anything else.

Soon as the attack was over, we didn't just stop shooting and then stand around. The adrenaline was flowing. We were back down in the magazine getting more ammunition, getting ready for the next wave. The Japanese came back after about half an hour. They stuck around a bit longer than the first wave. When the second wave came in, one bomb came at the *Honolulu* and was a near miss and hit the dock. It went down through the concrete before it went off. It caved the side of the ship in about four feet deep and about 20 feet high. The water flooded the magazines the same time it got hit.

Then there was hardly anything on our side of the ship to fire at. It was all over on the other side. We could see them hit Hickam Field, but they were just out of our range.

We stayed at our battle stations the rest of the day and all night. We were concerned, but I wasn't scared. There were all kinds of rumors around. Aircraft carriers out five miles, 10 miles. Paratroopers landing. Amphibious transports out there. The Japanese were all going to make a landing. Rumors flew like you would not believe. My concern that morning was where they had come from to get here so fast, and who declared war on who first."

AFTER the attack, Emory worked on convoys to Australia, was at the Battle of Tassafaronga, then served on an amphibious transport. He left the service in 1946, worked as a mechanical engineer, then moved back to Honolulu. Now 94, for the last 25 years he has worked with the Department of Defense to exhume and attempt to identify the remains of the more than 400 unidentified sailors and Marines killed aboard the U.S.S. *Oklahoma*. His tireless insistence on bringing closure to the families of the dead has resulted in the transferal of several remains home to their final resting place.

catastrophic nuclear devastation, nine countries are known to have nuclear warheads, only five of which are in accordance with the treaty: China, Russia, France, the U.K., and the U.S. India, Israel, and Pakistan never signed the treaty, and today they all possess nuclear arsenals and are pursuing new ballistic missile, cruise missile, and sea-based nuclear delivery systems. Perhaps of most urgent note is North Korea, which is hostile to the free world and ruled by a man universally deemed unstable.

What was the cost of victory? In April 2015, Japanese Prime Minister Shinzo Abe became the first of his office to address a joint meeting of Congress, standing in the very spot FDR had stood 74 years earlier to appeal for a declaration of war. Abe, who delivered his speech in English, spoke of his time as a student in California and his subsequent embrace of the values of democracy. He elaborated on the shared goals of the U.S.-Japanese "alliance of hope" to jointly tackle the new challenges of terrorism, infectious disease, natural disasters, and climate change, as well as "a proactive contribution to peace based on the principle of international cooperation." Aware of the intense scrutiny of his approach to Pearl Harbor, he visited the World War II Memorial before his speech and laid a wreath next to the Freedom Wall. As he told Congress, "I reflected upon the lost dreams and lost futures of these young Americans . . . with deep repentance in my heart, I stood there in silent prayers for some time. . . . My dear friends, on behalf of Japan and the Japanese people, I offer my profound respect and my eternal condolences to the souls of all American people that were lost during World War II."

▲ **SAILORS LINE THE DECK OF THE U.S.S. *CARL VINSON* TO HONOR their fallen comrades as the ship passes the *Arizona* Memorial in Pearl Harbor.**

▲ **ANY SURVIVING CREW MEMBER OF THE** *ARIZONA* **CAN CHOOSE** to have his remains interred near the number 4 gun turret to rejoin his comrades. To date, 38 have chosen that as their final resting place. Survivors of other ships can have their ashes scattered from the Memorial. Veterans of the attack are entitled to a full military funeral held on the Memorial for family, guests, and Pearl Harbor survivors. The Navy provides a rifle honor guard and a bugler. After the ceremony, divers deposit the urn containing the veteran's ashes into the sunken hull. Some survivors have lived into their hundreds and claim never to have replaced the friends they lost that day.

▶ **SERVICE MEMBERS STATIONED IN HAWAII REMAIN REVERENT** of the site, as both a mass grave and a potent reminder of the need for vigilance. During the government shutdown in 2013, they never considered abandoning their posts, continuing to tend the Memorial with the respect and dignity it will always command.

▼ **PARIS STARN, 6, PRAYS DURING THE MEMORIAL DAY SERVICE** at the National Memorial Cemetery of the Pacific in Honolulu on May 30, 2005.

And what of the souls of the more than 70,000 people who died immediately on August 6, 1945, when the *Enola Gay* released "Little Boy" over Hiroshima, incinerating part of the city and setting off raging fires? Over 30,000 more would die there by the end of the year. Or the more than 75,000 who would perish after the bombing of Nagasaki three days later? Robert Lewis, the co-pilot of the *Enola Gay*, had no inkling of the power of the bomb that the plane's crew dropped. Seeing the giant mushroom cloud and the pulverization of the city, he recorded in his flight log, "My God, what have we done?" For the Americans sitting down to dinner, unaware that their government had just wiped an entire city off the face of the planet, the news the following day was cause for celebration. The war was won; normal life could resume.

But today we know that normal life never did resume, that the existence of nuclear threat would change forever how we occupy our lives. Abe's "alliance of hope," however, offers a new paradigm. Just as many young Germans today decry the Nazi years, so does the new generation of Japanese rally for transparency and a global partnership for freedom and peace. Will we achieve universal accord, or did the bomb that ended World War II plant the seed for nuclear devastation? We look forward, hoping our politicians and citizens have learned the lessons taught by both Pearl Harbor and the nuclear destruction that followed.

CARL SHANEFF

▲ **THIS CLOCK WAS SALVAGED FROM THE *ARIZONA* IN 1942** and is now part of the U.S.S. *Arizona* Memorial, reflecting forever a heartbreaking moment.

▶ **THE IDEA FOR SOME KIND OF TESTIMONIAL TO HONOR THOSE** who perished during the attack on Pearl Harbor emerged in 1943 but wasn't realized until 1962 with the dedication of the U.S.S. *Arizona* Memorial. The 184-foot-long enclosed bridge spans the hull of the fallen battleship, whose name is synonymous with the events of December 7, 1941.